AS Business Studies
UNIT 2

OCR

Module 2872: Business Decisions

Roger Williams & Barry Martin

Philip Allan Updates
Market Place
Deddington
Oxfordshire
OX15 0SE

tel: 01869 338652
fax: 01869 337590
e-mail: sales@philipallan.co.uk
www.philipallan.co.uk

This Guide has been written specifically to support students preparing for the
OCR Business Studies Unit 2 examination. The content has been neither approved
nor endorsed by OCR and remains the sole responsibility of the authors.

Typeset by Alden Bookset, Oxford
Printed by Information Press, Eynsham, Oxford

Contents

Introduction

Content Guidance

Questions and Answers

Introduction

About this guide

This Student Unit Guide has been written with the aim of providing you with the ideal revision resource for OCR Unit 2, AS Business Studies. It is made up of three sections.

The first section, the **Introduction**, considers the nature and structure of the examination, the 'assessment unit'. It will help you to appreciate why the examination is structured in the way that it is, and this understanding will assist you in maximising your marks. Following a brief overview of the AS qualification, this section focuses upon the required skills and the key examination terms, concluding with revision and exam advice.

The second section, **Content Guidance**, considers the material that the examination is designed to cover. The examination only tests the content identified in the subject syllabus, the 'specification'. It is therefore important for you to know precisely what the examiners can test and what they cannot. In this way, you can devote your time and energy towards the material that is relevant. Links between different parts of the material within the specification will also be presented, with tips on ways to learn and understand the key content. You should not view this section as an alternative textbook or as a substitute for hard work in the lead up to the examination — this guide complements consistent study.

The third section, **Questions and Answers**, adopts the style of an answer critique. In this section, student answers are dissected and analysed so that their strengths and weaknesses can be identified. Through a benchmarking approach you can then seek to improve the quality of your answers so that examination marks are maximised.

Throughout this guide our focus is, unashamedly, on the objective of maximising your marks so that you can achieve the highest possible grade.

The aims and approach of the qualification

The consideration of issues in business studies is rarely confined to one, discrete, behavioural aspect of business — an integrated approach is required. For example, a marketing target may have both financial and human resource implications. The successful candidate should, therefore, be able to apply a range of knowledge and skills to the solution of business problems in a holistic manner.

OCR AS Business Studies aims to encourage candidates to:
- develop a critical understanding of organisations, the markets they serve and the process of adding value
- be aware that business behaviour can be studied from the perspectives of a range of stakeholders, including customers, managers, creditors, owners and employees

- demonstrate an understanding of the economic, environmental, ethical and international issues that arise as a consequence of business activity
- acquire a range of skills, including making decisions in the light of evaluation and, where appropriate, the quantification and management of information

Read these aims carefully. Your task in the examination is to demonstrate to the person who reads and marks your paper that you have acquired these skills. Reading the business section of a quality newspaper will help you achieve the first three of these aims.

Assessment

The AS qualification is designed to test certain skills. Consequently, in order to gain marks, candidates have to demonstrate these skills. The skills form a hierarchy, from 'knowledge' at the lowest level to 'evaluation' at the highest.
- **Knowledge** — the ability to recall accurately subject ideas and concepts.
- **Application** — bringing subject knowledge to bear on a situation.
- **Analysis** — the development of an argument which shows reasoning and a chain of logic using appropriate concepts and techniques of business studies.
- **Evaluation** — making a reasoned judgement having considered the available evidence critically.

You should note that the examiners will assume that demonstration of a higher skill implies the acquisition of lower skills, even though these lower skills may not be evident within the specific answer being assessed.

The proportion of marks for each skill varies slightly across the three assessment units which comprise the AS qualification. For this second unit — Business Decisions, 2872 — the overall weighting of the four skills across the whole examination paper is as follows:

Weighting

Knowledge	Level 1	(L1)	=	30%
Application	Level 2	(L2)	=	26⅔%
Analysis	Level 3	(L3)	=	23⅓%
Evaluation	Level 4	(L4)	=	20%

Suppose that a question is worth 10 marks. The L1 skill of knowledge is allocated 3 marks. Hence, demonstration of knowledge would gain a maximum of 3 marks. In contrast, because the skills are hierarchical, the demonstration of evaluation would gain some or all of the last 2 of the available marks, as well as all of the first 8 marks. Hence, if your answer contains evaluation, you will earn at least 9 marks out of the 10 available.

Your aim must be to demonstrate the highest possible level of skill as often as the examination requires. The mark you gain will reflect the skill within your answers — nothing more and nothing less.

Business Decisions, 2872

The subject content in the second module is examined in two different examination units: Business Decisions and Business Behaviour. This guide is written to address Business Decisions, 2872.

This module deals with the way in which businesses are organised and the way in which they operate. As such it builds upon the first module — Businesses: Their Objectives and Environment — simply because the way businesses operate is heavily influenced by the constraints and opportunities presented by their dynamic environment. The operation of businesses is the way in which they integrate the different functions within them so as to achieve their objectives. Consequently, as stated in the specification:

> Candidates should be able to recognise interrelationships between each of the four main behavioural functions of business and that for an organisation to be a success in a dynamic and challenging environment decisions have to be taken in the context of both the organisation's wider objectives and resources.

Because of the way the OCR AS qualification is designed, the examiner will assume that you have covered the first module, Businesses: Their Objectives and Environment, 2871, regardless of whether or not you have sat the unit examination. Questions in the Business Decisions unit can cover the content of both modules. There might be a question, or part question, specifically about content from the first module. However, even if the questions do not explicitly ask about the earlier module, you should seek to show your grasp of it in your answers. This means you need to revise work from the first module for this examination.

Key examination words

Each examination question can be broken down into two parts. One part is the key verb, which is the instruction as to the top level of skill involved. This verb, together with the mark allocation, will indicate the highest skill expected by the examiners. The other part of the question will identify the specific subject area to be tested.

Suppose the following question was set: 'Identify three factors which will influence the price charged by a business.' As the key verb is **identify**, the examiner is only expecting an answer which demonstrates knowledge of the subject area being tested: determinants of price. A change in the key verb significantly changes the skill required. 'Discuss three factors which will determine the price charged by a business', is an altogether different question. Here the key verb, **discuss**, would indicate that the examiner is expecting a full consideration of three factors, with detailed reasoning as to which factor is the most important (it would be the context of the case study which would enable you to make this judgement).

In order to maximise marks, you need to identify both the key verb and the subject area before answering the question.

Within discursive examination questions, the following key verbs indicate precisely what the examiner is looking for and the highest skill level being tested.

Analyse	L3	develop a full and detailed argument
Assess	L4	consider the value for or against a particular point
Comment	L2	give a brief explanation
Define	L1	give the precise meaning of the term or concept
Describe	L2	give a detailed account of an issue or concept
Discuss	L4	consider through argument
Evaluate	L4	offer a reasoned judgement
Explain how	L2	give an accurate account
Explain why	L3	give detailed reasoning
Justify	L4	develop a fully reasoned argument that supports a view
Outline	L2	give an account of the main features
Recommend	L4	come to a supported position through detailed argument
State	L1	make a series of unsupported points

Calculations and formulae

You need to take a careful approach when answering a question that involves a calculation:

- If you state a formula, this demonstrates knowledge at L1.
- If you insert data from the case study into the formula that you have stated and then perform the calculation to find the answer, this demonstrates the skill of application at L2.
- If you interpret the outcome of the calculation, this demonstrates analysis at L3.

It is a mistake to think that you should use statistical information only when the question specifically asks for it. By using a calculation to aid the interpretation of data, you demonstrate the ability to engage in analysis and, as a consequence, you would gain over half of the available marks.

Opportunities for evaluation

You can now see that high marks arise from analysis and evaluation. The most obvious and likely way to demonstrate evaluation is through reasoned discussion. Reasoned discussion often contains certain phrases and terms that, typically, will help construct an evaluative answer. The phrases and terms which encourage a balanced view include:

- In the short run ... but in the longer term ...
- This issue/factor is more important because ...
- Doing this would result in ... because ...
- Whether or not depends upon ...
- In addition, the following needs to be considered because ...
- Internally such a change would ... but externally the following might ...

When seeking to evaluate a situation to gain high marks, you need to consider the reasons *why* a business or an individual behaves in the way described. Businesses and individuals act in ways that they feel will help them achieve their objectives. Therefore, in seeking to evaluate, you should consider the likely objectives so that you can give a fully reasoned discussion that addresses the question 'why?'

The main areas for potential evaluation within the second unit include the following:
- Under what circumstances might a product-oriented business be successful?
- Could a selling — rather than a marketing — approach be appropriate?
- Do marketing concepts such as 'product life-cycle' have any validity?
- Are samples worthwhile if the results cannot be considered as accurate?
- Isn't it the case that cost is the most important consideration in setting price?
- Does the concept of elasticity have any value given that its underlying assumptions are so unrealistic?
- Are cash flow and asset utilisation more important than profit as a means of ensuring survival?
- Faced with a dynamic environment, do budgets serve any function in business?
- Are raw material costs the only true variable costs?
- If a firm cannot do anything about fixed costs, can they be ignored?
- What role, if any, might financial accounting have in business decision-making?
- Which investment appraisal is the best?
- Is a balance sheet — given its level of detail — of any real use to stakeholders?
- Are people the most important business resource?
- Is employment law a constraint on business behaviour?
- Why might a business not train its workforce?
- If employees are told what to do and are supervised, does their motivation matter?
- Could payment by results (PBR) be the best way to reward employees?
- Isn't delegation just a manager's way of getting someone else to do his or her job for no extra money?
- Is there a place for autocratic leadership in modern business?
- Does size matter?
- Should a business worry about the waste produced from its processes?
- Is working at maximum output always desirable?
- If a firm has no competition, is it worth worrying about quality?
- Should a firm hold buffer stock?

This list is by no means exhaustive. Rather, its purpose is to encourage a questioning approach to the material within the module. Such an approach will mean you are better able to construct a reasoned argument that supports a particular position.

Revision planning

The way you plan your revision is essentially down to personal preference, as what may work for one individual may not work for another. However, there are common principles of revision that lead to examination success:

- Start your revision in plenty of time. This means you need to know the date of the examination well in advance.
- Ensure that your notes and files are complete.
- Ensure you have an appropriate textbook and identify which sections are relevant by checking against your scheme of work.
- Arrange to have somewhere quiet and comfortable to work. Try to avoid being disturbed while you are studying.
- Set yourself a series of short-term goals within an overall revision schedule.
- Reward yourself as you reach short-term goals by taking some brief time away from revision.
- Work in short, intense bursts. Quality of revision is as important as quantity.
- Reread your notes. Jotting down the essential points as you read will help maintain concentration. Think of using mind maps/diagrams rather than pages of longhand to reinforce key points.
- Make a note of any areas of uncertainty so you can ask for clarification later.
- Practise writing answers to examination questions without your notes and within the time limit of the examination.
- Check your answers to ensure that they contain the appropriate order skills indicated by the key verbs in the questions.

Examination success

Sitting examinations can be a stressful experience. However, stress can be alleviated by appropriate preparation. As a minimum you will need to:
- know the date, time and location of the examination
- arrive at least 10 minutes before the scheduled start time
- ensure that you have all of your examination equipment, i.e. black pens, pencils, and a ruler and calculator
- become familiar with the examination format (the examination board issues a specimen paper and mark scheme)
- know what you can achieve in the time permitted
- make sure you write clearly, using sentences that are not too long and clumsy

The examiner's demands

The format of the examination is a data–response paper. Each question will take the form of a short piece of business material upon which questions are based. It is highly likely that there will be an explicit numerate requirement in a question. Consequently, you must have a calculator which you are able to use with confidence.

The data–response format is different to the case study format (Unit 1, Businesses: Their Objectives and Environment) in both demand and style. The material will be brief and explicitly directed toward the tools and concepts being examined. The material in the piece will need to be interpreted and manipulated — skills you will have developed throughout the course.

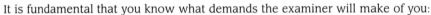

It is fundamental that you know what demands the examiner will make of you:
- The examination lasts 75 minutes.
- It will have two compulsory questions, each subdivided. In turn, all parts of questions are compulsory.
- The maximum number of marks is 60 (including 2 marks for 'quality of written communication').
- The questions will be based on a short piece of data. The examiner will expect you to use this as evidence within your answers.

Both of the two questions are compulsory, so there is no advantage or disadvantage in doing them in any order. However, there is real advantage in answering the whole question in the order of the parts, i.e. **once you have decided which question to start with you should complete the entire question, working from part (a) through to part (d)**. This is because of the way in which the part questions can interrelate with each other. An earlier part question could provide new evidence for subsequent parts, which was not in the data given by the examiner. For example, the answer to a calculation in part (b) may provide useful evidence for the major discursive question, part (d).

Begin by carefully reading the verbal data. While you read, identify which aspects are fact and which are opinion. Opinions are important, but they need to be treated with more care than facts if you later use these to support your answer. Then examine any numerate data, whether in the form of a table, graphs or charts. Next, read the questions, noting the key verb. Having read the data and the questions, you should be able to identify the area of the specification that is being assessed and the tools and concepts you will need to draw upon to answer the questions effectively.

Allow yourself about 5 minutes to understand the data fully. Only then start answering the questions. As you read them, note the mark allocation. Working at a pace of 1 mark per minute will mean you can complete the examination with a few minutes to review your answers.

Content
Guidance

The content divides into the four main behavioural functions of business:
- Marketing (page 13)
- Accounting and finance (page 24)
- People in organisations (page 36)
- Operations management (page 40)

Each of the four behaviours integrates with the other three. Consequently, the content should be studied as an integrative whole, approaching business decisions from a variety of perspectives. Similarly, your answers should draw upon issues from across the four behaviours, rather than being confined to a single one. We will show you opportunities for integration in this section.

Although all the module content is examinable, the data–response method of assessment has influenced how the content can be examined. The structure of the examination means that the focus will be on the tools and concepts which businesses use in making decisions. You need to be able to employ these decision tools in a wide variety of contexts so that you can use them appropriately in the exam. Make sure that you can evaluate the use of a decision tool and have a clear appreciation of its advantages and limitations.

Within this section we suggest how the examiner might construct a question on each particular piece of content. **These suggestions should not be regarded as the only way in which the content might be assessed — they are intended as examples.** As will be clear, it is entirely possible to assess much of the content through data–response questions and not just those few explicitly numerical techniques, e.g. breakeven analysis.

Your aim in reading this section should be to develop your higher order skills. One way to develop these skills even further would be to practise answering the examination-style questions given in the third section of this guide.

Marketing

The market, its definition and structure

A market can be defined as a place, either real or virtual, where organisations meet their customers to engage in voluntary exchange to their mutual benefit.

Marketing is concerned with finding and satisfying customers so that both the firm and its customers benefit from their transaction. The process of marketing ensures that the business is able to organise its resources efficiently to provide the required good or service, in the right quantity, at a suitable price, through a distribution channel that is convenient to both itself and its customers. Consequently, there are several different aspects to the marketing function, each of which has to be integrated appropriately to achieve success.

The management of the marketing process is a vital ingredient in ensuring the achievement of the business's objectives. Selling to customers ultimately provides the business with its revenue, and in the long run and in the private sector, revenue has to exceed total cost to create a profit, thus ensuring that the business survives.

Marketing objectives are converted into marketing strategies. These are the long-term plans that set out which resources are to be coordinated to achieve the objective. These strategies are, in turn, converted into marketing tactics. These set out in detail what has to be done, by whom, by when, so that the objective is achieved. Thus, in the long run, marketing objectives have to be compatible with the organisation's overall objectives. The table below shows potential links between business objectives and marketing behaviour.

Overall objective	Possible marketing strategy
Profit	Price to exceed total cost Find an uncontested niche
Survival	Price to generate cash flow Enter new market Cut back on expenditure
Growth	Low price to boost sales High levels of promotion Find new customer segment
Prestige	High-quality products Branding New products/innovation

Evaluation The ability to define a market accurately is crucial to the proper use of marketing tools and concepts. By redefining their market, firms can refocus their efforts and target the appropriate audience more accurately. For example, the way in which electricity producers define their market will influence their behaviour and approach. If they see their market as electricity, they will be less concerned with the actions of a gas company. Redefining their market as domestic energy makes the gas company a direct competitor.

Market segmentation

We can divide markets into segments. A market segment is a portion of the whole market with unique characteristics. Examples include segmentation by age, gender, location, lifestyle, occupation and socioeconomic group.

Evaluation The segmentation used will reflect the product being offered and the customers' needs. For example, age and income would be a key means of market segmentation in financial services, whereas location would be of less importance.

Question
From data, identify and divide a market into segments. Suggest how the firm might exploit the characteristics of each segment to its maximum benefit.

Market size

The size of a market can be measured both in terms of volume, i.e. by units sold, and by value, i.e. by sales revenue. A market can remain static in terms of volume but grow in terms of value due to inflation or price increases.

Link Go to Unit 1.

Question
From sales data, determine the size of a market. Analyse whether the size of the market has changed because of sales volume or value and how the firm might react accordingly.

Market growth

Through time, a market might grow for several reasons. Market growth can be measured by comparing the size of the market at two points in time. Typically, this is done year-on-year and expressed as a percentage.

Link Go to Unit 1 for the determinants of demand.

Evaluation Growing markets present firms with opportunities. Hence, marketing behaviour will be aggressive in capturing sales. In contrast, a contracting market means adopting a defensive posture to protect existing sales from competitors.

Question
From data, calculate the percentage increase in market size, either in total or as an annual value. Suggest what opportunities such growth presents for the firm, and what decisions it might take to exploit this growth to its advantage.

Market share

An organisation compares its market share of sales with that of the entire market, in terms of either volume or value. The formula is:

$$\frac{\text{company sales}}{\text{market sales}} \times 100\%$$

Market share can change either because of changes in market size, or because the firm's sales levels are changing, or a combination of both, as shown below.

		Market size		
		Growing	*Static*	*Contracting*
Firm's sales	*Growing*	No change	Increasing	Increasing
	Static	Decreasing	No change	Increasing
	Contracting	Decreasing	Decreasing	No change

Evaluation Decisions taken about a product on the basis of changed market share should reflect the reasons for the change, not merely the change itself. Market share can change due to factors beyond the control of the business and so it may be entirely appropriate to maintain current marketing efforts.

Question
From data, calculate the firm's market share. Suggest reasons why it might be changing and what decisions the firm might take to gain or preserve market share.

Market research and analysis

In order to understand the market, the firm may engage in market research, either through primary or secondary data.

Primary data

Primary data are collected for the firm's specific purpose. Although the firm may use a specialist market researcher to collect the information, it is able to direct the research. Primary research therefore has a high degree of relevance for the firm. However, it can be expensive, in terms of both time and cash.

Primary research tools include:
- observation
- interviews
- focus groups
- questionnaires

Secondary data

Secondary data have already been collected for some other purpose. This means they are often cheaper to assemble. However, they are often dated and of marginal validity for the firm's purpose. Suitable secondary data offer a quick and inexpensive overview of the market. Detail can be added by conducting subsequent primary research in the light of the secondary findings.

Quantitative and qualitative data

Quantitative data use numbers to measure aspects of the market, e.g. how often someone purchases a particular brand. Manipulating and summarising quantitative data can be straightforward.

Qualitative data assess the attitudes and motivations which lie behind the purchasing decisions of respondents. Because the outcome is verbal, such data can be difficult to manipulate and summarise.

Question

Manipulate data, either quantitative or qualitative, to generate an analytical summary. Suggest how the outcome of market research could be used to inform decision-makers about a marketing plan.

Sampling

Sampling is collecting data from a part of the overall population that is assumed to be typical of the whole. Investigating a representative cross-section rather than the whole population saves time, money and effort.

Sampling introduces the risk that the data collected do not give a true and fair reflection of the whole population. Various methods of sampling can be used to minimise this risk. The larger the sample chosen, the greater the chance that it is a fair cross-section of the population, but the more resources will be needed to collect the data.

Random sampling

Every member of the population has an equal chance of being questioned. Such samples are difficult to manage and are most appropriate where it is difficult to identify differences within the population. Where there are differences, other methods can be used that break up the population.

Quota sampling

A predetermined number of respondents are questioned. This method is often allied to segmentation so that set numbers of respondents are questioned within different groups. This produces a stratified quota sample.

Systematic sampling

Respondents are chosen using a predetermined interval, e.g. every tenth person.

Cluster sampling

Respondents are drawn from a particular location.

Question

Analyse the validity of a particular set of market research data. Discuss its appropriateness in terms of size, methodology and type of sample. Suggest how the outcome of market research could be used to inform decision-makers about how the firm should go forward to achieve its objective.

Evaluation The findings of market research are open to doubt. This is because:
- The methodology used may be flawed, e.g. sample size is too small.
- Respondents may not be truthful, e.g. they may tell you what they think you want to hear rather than what they really think.
- Market conditions may change, e.g. social changes and economic factors.
- Markets may become saturated so that growth or trends cannot continue indefinitely.
- Competitor actions may make findings irrelevant.
- There may be difficulties in identifying causal relationships, e.g. have sales risen because of advertising or because of competitor price changes?

Marketing planning

This involves the formulation of marketing objectives, strategies for their implementation and tactics. Marketing objectives set out how the marketing department should contribute to the overall organisational objectives. Further, the marketing objectives will be set in the light of analysis of the firm's current position and prevailing and anticipated environmental influences.

Link Go to Unit 1.

Marketing strategies

Marketing strategies set out the marketing behaviour that is required to achieve the marketing objectives. There are four main examples of a marketing strategy.

Mass versus niche marketing

This type of strategy identifies the target, either by treating the market as a whole or by aiming at specific sub-groups within a larger market.

Product portfolio analysis

A portfolio analysis creates a coherent balance of products that addresses the needs of the target group while ensuring the organisation can achieve its objectives.

Life-cycle analysis

Life-cycle analysis is the creation of a series of products at different stages in the product life cycle so that those in maturity provide funds for those in their early stages.

Differentiated marketing

This type of marketing strategy makes products which are different to those of potential and actual competitors. It requires the establishment of clear brand identities and values, or the creation of products with intrinsic or imagined unique selling propositions (USPs). Differentiated marketing allows the firm to charge higher prices because of the customers' perception of the increased value of the products offered.

> **Evaluation** The success of a firm's marketing strategy depends on many factors:
> - The business's ability to analyse the needs of its customers correctly.
> - The business's ability to analyse the external environment accurately, both as it is and how it will change in the future (see Unit 1).
> - The ability of the whole organisation to act as a single entity.
> - Whether the finance department releases the required funding for a promotional campaign.
> - Whether the operations department is successful in delivering the required quantity and quality of product on time.
> - Whether the personnel department delivers effective training programmes so that staff are able to explain to customers the benefits of new products.
>
> The last three of the above show how other departments' behaviour affects the achievement of marketing objectives. This list is by no means exhaustive and you should be able to think of other examples.

The marketing plan

The establishment of a marketing strategy leads to the creation of the marketing plan. The 4Ps of the marketing mix (product, price, place and promotion) provide the framework for the elements of the marketing plan. It is important that each element integrates and complements the other for a coherent marketing plan to emerge.

■ Product

This describes the offering to the customer, and can be anything from a physical item to an intangible service. Product purchases by customers provide the business with its income. Without an attractive product to offer, the business will be unsuccessful in generating the revenue it needs to cover costs and make profits.

Product development

This is the process whereby the business translates the identification of customer needs into products that effectively meet such needs. An equally important consideration in this process is ensuring that the developed product can be provided within the constraints of existing resources and while delivering the required return on capital employed.

Product life cycle

This describes the stages, in terms of sales volumes, that a product goes through from initial idea to withdrawal from the market. The position of the product within its life cycle will have an influence upon the marketing tactics employed, as shown in the table below.

	Introduction	Growth	Maturity	Decline
Pricing	Low to penetrate market, or high to recoup R&D costs	Aggressive to beat competition	Defensive to maintain volumes	Price for profit, not volume
Promotion	Create awareness Educate	Create/ strengthen brand	Maintain loyalty, reinforcement	Little expenditure
Place	Exclusive/selective	Broaden links to channel	Intensive, keep channel supplied	Phase out marginal channels

Because products in the mature phase of the life cycle are net generators of cash, efforts are required to maintain the length of this phase. These methods are called extension strategies and include:

- finding new markets
- finding new uses
- encouraging more frequent usage
- launching associated products
- making minor modifications, restyling, adding additional features

Cash flows from mature products are used to develop new products and to subsidise those in the initial stages of the life cycle while they become established.

A further reason for wishing to extend the life of a product is that it might be a key element of a range of products that, if it were prematurely discontinued, might negatively impact upon the rest of the products within the range.

Question

Analyse sales data by inspection/graphing to identify the stage of a product in its life cycle. Make decisions about amendments to the marketing plan to ensure the product continues to deliver benefit to the firm.

The Boston matrix

This is a tool that analyses the position of a product in two dimensions. The first is in terms of its market share relative to other products in the same market. The second is the rate of growth within the market.

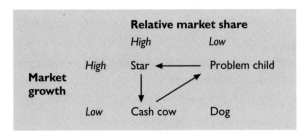

Cash cows can be used to develop today's stars and problem children so that they become the cash cows of the future. Products classified as dogs should be discontinued unless they support other products as complements.

Question

Analyse sales and market data to determine the position of product(s) within the Boston matrix. Make decisions about appropriate marketing plans in the light of the position of the products.

■ Price

Price is the only element of the business's marketing plan which yields income. The others are all costs. Cost — along with competition and the customer base — are the three considerations in setting price.

Cost

In the long run, price must exceed unit cost if a profit is to be gained.

Competition

In competitive markets, with low levels of brand loyalty and product differentiation, the firm will have to set price in line with those of the competition to maintain sales.

Customer

The willingness of customers to purchase at a given price will influence the final price set. Customers' ability and willingness to pay will reflect their perception of the product's value, their income and the opportunity cost of purchase.

> **Link** There is a clear link between pricing and the consideration of the business's external environment as studied in Unit 1, particularly supply and demand as well as the social and economic environments.

Pricing methods

The three pricing methods are full cost, contribution and discrimination.

Full cost pricing

This is the addition of a suitable margin above full cost, sometimes called 'cost-plus' pricing. It requires a knowledge of the cost base and is most often used in retailing.

Contribution pricing

This is when the price covers the marginal costs of production so that any surplus can assist in the payment of fixed costs. It enables low prices to be set for short periods of time or for particular circumstances, e.g. special orders and spare capacity.

Discrimination pricing

This sets different prices for different customers for essentially the same good. It requires the ability to divide the market into segments with different price sensitivities and to keep each segment separate from the others.

Question

From cost and market data, suggest a suitable price for a given product. Make decisions about appropriate marketing plans in the light of the price and how the other elements of the marketing plan could be integrated.

Pricing tactics

Promotional pricing

This means setting the price lower than that of competitors. The aim is to increase sales in the expectation of making additional full price sales for other products. It is typically used in retailing, where the 'loss leader' generates increased traffic volumes through the store and so exposes customers to many other fully priced offerings.

Psychological pricing

Psychological pricing is where the price is set to reflect the expectations of the customer. For example, a high price may enhance the customer's impression of quality. An offer price — setting the price below a key psychological boundary, e.g. £9.99 rather than £10 — enhances the customer's impression of value.

Pricing strategies

Skimming

Skimming sets an initially high price to recoup costs and is often used in the early stages of the product's life and before competitors enter the market. It allows for recovery of R&D costs before competition forces defensive price-cutting.

Penetration pricing

This sets an aggressively low price to capture market share upon entry into the market.

An alternative use of penetration pricing is as a means of setting a low price to dissuade potential competitors from entering the market due to low returns.

Predatory pricing

Predatory pricing sets prices at a low level to drive the competition out of the market. Once the competition has left the market, prices may be raised to recoup the income lost while engaged in the price battle.

Question

From cost and market data, suggest a suitable pricing strategy for a given product. Make decisions about appropriate marketing plans in the light of the price and how the other elements of the marketing plan could be integrated.

Price elasticity of demand

Price elasticity of demand (PED) measures the sensitivity of changes in customer demand given a change in price. It is assumed that the observed change in demand is solely due to a change in price of the product. The formula for PED is:

$$\frac{\% \text{ change in quantity demanded}}{\% \text{ change in price}}$$

If PED is:

- Greater than 1, customers are price sensitive — any change in price will lead to a proportionately larger change in demand and a reduction in price will result in increased revenue.
- Equal to 1, any change in price will lead to the same change in demand such that revenues will not alter.
- Less than 1, customers are price insensitive — any change in price will lead to a proportionately smaller change in demand and a reduction in price will result in decreased revenue.

The factors that affect PED are:

- time — sensitivity increases as more time passes since the change in price
- habit — habitual purchasers are less sensitive to price changes
- income — the greater the proportion of income the purchase of a product requires, the more price sensitive customers will be
- substitutes — customers who perceive the product to have no substitutes will be less price sensitive

Question

From price and demand data, calculate and interpret price sensitivity. Suggest what decisions a business might take in the light of knowledge about customers' sensitivity to changes in price. Make decisions about appropriate marketing plans in the light of PED and how the other elements of the marketing plan could be integrated.

Evaluation Elasticity is only useful as a decision tool when the firm has accurate information regarding the demand curve for the product. The value of market research in this regard is limited by the inherent weaknesses of the research. Similarly, the demand curve can only be determined from experience if the environment has not changed since that experience, something of an unlikelihood given the dynamic environment in which businesses operate.

■ Place

Place describes the channel of distribution the product takes from producer to customer. To be successful, the producer has to persuade both the final consumer as well as the channel intermediaries of the benefit of its products. The needs of these two groups are different, and consequently the message and techniques used to communicate with them will also be different.

Channel intermediaries

Channel intermediaries might be persuaded about the product by high margins, dealer support, or reduced risk through sale or return. The traditional distribution channel in consumer markets is:

producer ⟶ wholesaler ⟶ retailer ⟶ customer

Channel intermediaries enable manufacturing in high volumes and selling in smaller quantities. They also allow geographically diverse markets to be served. The more channel intermediaries, the more the available profit is shared out, and the less the direct contact with the consumer. Improvements in information and communications technology (ICT) enable firms to discuss and sell direct, e.g. e-commerce and internet shopping.

Question
Analyse channel data to suggest a suitable route for a given product. Make decisions about appropriate marketing plans in the light of the place and how the other elements of the marketing plan could be integrated.

■ Promotion

Above the line

Above-the-line promotion communicates with customers and potential customers through media, e.g. print, electronic.

Below the line

Below-the-line promotion communicates with customers and potential customers through sales promotions, sponsorship, etc.

Promotional activities

Whether above or below the line, promotion is concerned with communicating with the customer. To be effective, the firm has to understand the customers' needs and motivations for purchase. Promotion is a series of integrated activities, which together have to form a coherent message. The aim of promotion is to encourage eventual sales, but its immediate focus can include:

- education — informing customers about products, particularly new ones
- persuasion — attempting to get customers to purchase
- awareness — telling customers of the product's attributes and availability

Evaluation To be effective, promotion should lead to increased sales in a cost-effective manner. This requires the firm to know with whom it wishes to communicate and the appropriate media for contact. Further, it is necessary to be able to assess effectiveness by measuring sales both before and after promotion.

Link Fluctuating sales levels may not be due to any promotional action taken by the firm but rather due to environmental changes (see Unit 1).

Question
From cost and media data, suggest a suitable promotional mix in a given situation. Analyse data to determine whether a particular promotional mix is appropriate in the light of aims and resources. Make decisions about appropriate marketing plans in the light of the promotional method and how the other elements of the marketing plan could be integrated.

Accounting and finance

Accounting and finance, by their very nature, make extensive use of numerical data and together form a rich area for data–response questions. This section of the specification can be divided into two parts: management accounting and financial accounting.

Management accounting

Management accounting provides accounting information to decision-makers. This aspect is essentially forward-looking and internal. It is concerned with the analysis of data used to make decisions, so that possible implications can be assessed before the decision is made.

Financial accounting

Financial accounting summarises what has happened in the business. As such, its focus is historic and external. However, experience and historic data can be important when making decisions. For example, financial accounting can be useful in monitoring and controlling the use of scarce financial resources. Hence, this is an equally important area of study.

Budgets

A budget is a quantifiable plan for a defined period of time. Examples include quarterly materials budgets, monthly overtime budgets etc. Budgets are useful for:

- setting targets, i.e. what has to be achieved?
- measuring success, i.e. has the target been met?
- communication of targets, i.e. informing people of what they need to achieve
- coordination, i.e. ensuring that everyone is working to the same end and that resources are appropriately allocated
- controlling use of resources, i.e. ensuring performance remains within acceptable bounds
- monitoring performance, i.e. the budget provides a basis for achievement
- allocating responsibility, i.e. identifying who has to do what, by when

Setting the budget

There are two means of establishing a budget: zero (or base) budgeting and historic budgeting.

Zero (base) budgeting
Each item of resource has to be individually justified before its allocation. This encourages managers to plan and to anticipate how much of the business's overall resources they need to meet their goals. By their nature, zero-based budgets are set in conjunction with supervisors. This will encourage managers to see the budget as something they have drawn up, and so there are clear motivational implications.

Historic budgeting
Resource allocation is based upon the amount given in previous years. For example, a department might be given a budget that is 4% more than last year. One possible disadvantage is that this approach may encourage the consumption of resources towards the end of the budgetary period to provide evidence of the need for more resources in the next period.

Subdividing the budget

Budgets can be set at various levels within a business. For instance, an overall budget could be divided into the four behavioural areas of the business. A marketing budget could be divided into sub-activities, e.g. sponsorship and advertising. As the budget is subdivided, the level of detail within it becomes greater. The parts of a business that have budgets can be described as **cost centres** and **profit centres**.

Cost centre
An area of a business to which costs can be allocated, e.g. department, person or activity.

Profit centre
An area of a business that both generates revenues and incurs costs.

Budget variance
After setting a budgetary target, performance towards its achievement can be monitored and assessed. Any difference between actual and budget achievement is known as a variance, and can be either favourable or adverse.

Favourable variance
A favourable budget variance results in profits that are higher than forecast.

Adverse variance
An adverse budget variance results in reduced profits that are lower than forecast.

Impact of budget variances

	Revenue	Cost
Budget > actual	Adverse	Favourable
Budget < actual	Favourable	Adverse

Coping with an adverse variance
Where necessary, corrective action can be initiated if there is going to be a difference between the budget plan and actual achievement. Further, the underlying cause of the variance can be investigated. This enables responsibility to be allocated appropriately. For example, a materials budget may be adverse because of an increase in the prices a supplier charges. In this case, the manager can do little. However, a materials budget may be adverse because of poor utilisation, something which the manager might be expected to rectify.

Question
From data, construct a budget. Then, interpret variances and suggest what decisions might be appropriate in the light of the analysis.

Link Budget variances can be caused by changes in the business's external environment: see Unit 1. For example, reduced unemployment might necessitate a higher than expected wage rise so that actual wage costs exceed budgeted wage costs. Budgets also link to motivation and leadership.

Evaluation The value of a budget as a motivational tool depends upon the degree of employee participation in drawing it up. Further, managers can only be held accountable for factors over which they have control. To criticise a manager for an adverse variance caused by an external change may lead to demotivation. Similarly, the value of a budget will depend upon the degree of change in the firm's environment.

Cash flow

Cash

Cash is the most liquid of a business's assets. It is needed to meet the day-to-day debts of the business.

Too little cash

Holding too little cash could result in:
- a creditor refusing to supply
- not being able to pay wages
- business failure

Too much cash

Holding too much cash carries an opportunity cost in that the cash is an idle resource. Long-term spare cash would, for example, be better spent on purchasing a new machine. Short-term spare cash could be placed in an interest-bearing bank account. Hence, managing cash flow is a balance between having enough for immediate use and not having wasteful excess.

Optimising cash

Cash can be optimised by:
- ensuring debtors are prompt in their payments
- factoring debtors to receive partial payment more quickly
- delaying payment of invoices until the due date
- not building up excessive levels of stock
- taking credit terms if these do not result in increased prices
- renting rather than buying an asset if it is only needed in the short term

Cash budgets

To manage cash flow, businesses construct cash budgets. These can be used to anticipate shortages of cash so that action can be planned, e.g. negotiating a bank loan for the period of the shortfall.

The structure of a cash budget

Cash inflow	Credit sales + Cash sales + Other inflows, e.g. disposal of unwanted assets, sale of shares etc.
Less cash outflow	Purchases + Wages + Utilities + Rent etc. + Other outflows, e.g. paying an insurance premium, paying dividends etc.
=	Net cash flow for the period, e.g. month
+	Opening cash (the closing balance of the previous period)
=	Closing cash

Actions to manage cash flow

Shortfalls of cash can be managed by:

- delaying outflows
- reducing outflows
- speeding up inflows
- increasing inflows
- borrowing, i.e. arranging an overdraft or a short-term loan

The action taken to manage cash flow will reflect the underlying cause of any cash flow problem. An immediate shortage of cash requires a different response to an emerging pattern of reduced cash balances. If, for example, the business is increasingly short of cash due to poor sales, it might be appropriate to reduce prices or change promotional tactics. However, a temporary shortage at the end of the month may require the use of an overdraft.

Question
From data, construct a cash budget. Suggest what decisions might be required to optimise the use of cash in the light of the analysis.

Costs

Costs can be described by their behaviour or by their allocation.

Costs by behaviour

Fixed costs (FC)
Also known as overheads, fixed costs do not change with output in the short run, e.g. rent, salaries.

Variable costs (VC)
Variable costs change directly, often proportionately, with output, e.g. raw materials. As output rises, so does the total variable cost (TVC), i.e. TVC is VC per unit × the number of units produced (Q).

Marginal costs (MC)
This expresses the change in total cost with a change in output. Marginal cost can be either variable, e.g. to make another unit more raw materials are required, or fixed, e.g. to make another unit a bigger machine is required.

Total cost (TC)
Total cost is the combined cost at any level of output, so TC = FC + TVC. As output rises, so will total cost. However, average total cost (ATC) will fall as output rises as fixed costs are spread across more units: ATC = TC/output.

content guidance

Costs by allocation

Direct costs
A cost that can be specifically attributed to a particular part of the business (product, department, cost centre), e.g. manufacturing staff wages.

Indirect costs
A cost that cannot be specifically attributed to a particular part of the business (product, department, cost centre), e.g. corporate hospitality.

Overheads
A cost that does not arise directly from the process of creating the business's output, e.g. office staff salaries.

A cost can be both variable and indirect. Similarly, a cost can be both fixed and direct. The description of the cost is the way in which it is managed rather than its size. Businesses need to allocate costs to different cost centres to enable the benefit of each part of the business to be assessed. Therefore, for example, a firm producing three products would have to divide its rent bill (an indirect cost) across the three production departments, so that it knows the unit cost of making each product. This information will in turn enable the business to set a realistic price for the product. However, a different method of allocating costs will yield a different unit cost.

Total profit

Total profit is calculated as: profit = sales revenue − total cost.

On a unit basis: profit = price − unit cost.

Contribution costing

Because it is revenue minus total cost, the calculation of profit includes both fixed and variable costs. However, because a business cannot change its fixed costs in the short run, it is possible to disregard them in some circumstances. This approach is called contribution costing.

Contribution is calculated as: contribution = sales revenue – total variable cost.

On a unit basis: contribution per unit = price – average variable cost.

The situations when a contribution approach would be appropriate are special orders and make or buy decisions.

Special orders
Suppose a business has some spare manufacturing capacity and receives an enquiry from a customer to make an order at £12. The normal price of the item, £15, is calculated as: variable costs = £10; fixed cost = £4; profit = £1.

Whether the firm takes the order or not, it still has to pay the fixed costs and as such these do not affect the decision. Providing the order exceeds the variable costs, it will generate a surplus that will help pay some of the fixed costs. In this example, the order is worth taking because it yields £2 of contribution to fixed costs.

This approach is useful provided that:
● other customers do not demand a similarly reduced price
● supplying this customer does not lead to cancelled orders from other customers
● the additional order can be made without changing any other costs

Make or buy decisions
Suppose a business that has spare capacity receives an offer from a firm wanting to supply a part it normally makes for itself. Should it buy in the part? The cost of the part the business makes is: variable costs = £8; fixed cost = £2.

Provided that the offer is for less than £8, it should be accepted because this is less than the variable cost of manufacture.

Suppose the firm was operating at full capacity. If the offer is for £9, it is worth accepting providing the released capacity can be switched to make an item which yields more than £1 contribution (the difference between £9 and £8) in the time it would have taken to make the part.

Question
From data, calculate contribution. Decide the best action for the firm in the light of the contribution and the given situation.

Breakeven

The concept of contribution is used in determining breakeven. Breakeven describes the level of output where total revenue = total cost, i.e. the business makes neither profits nor losses. Operating above breakeven means the business will make profits.

In contrast, operating below breakeven means the business will make losses.

The formula for breakeven is:

$$\text{output} = \frac{\text{fixed cost}}{\text{contribution per unit}}$$

For example, in a firm with fixed costs of £1,000 per month where the price of one unit is £7.50 and its variable costs are £5.00, how many units does it need to make and sell to break even? Solution:

$$\text{output} = \frac{£1,000}{£7.50 - £5.00} = 400 \text{ units}$$

The breakeven level of output can be reduced by:
- increasing prices
- reducing variable cost per unit
- reducing fixed cost

The calculation of breakeven requires certain assumptions. These are:
- costs are either fixed or variable
- fixed costs remain constant across a range of output
- there is no change to the variable cost of each unit of output
- all units are sold at the same price
- all of the output manufactured in a period is sold in that period

Breakeven can also be used to determine the price that needs to be charged at a certain level of output to make a target level of profit. This is achieved by adding the target profit to the total cost at the desired level of profit. This figure is the target revenue. The price required is found by dividing the target revenue by the number of units to be sold.

Margin of safety

The margin of safety is calculated as follows:

margin of safety = current output – breakeven output

This measure shows how far sales can fall before the business will make losses. Suppose, in the above example, the firm is selling 500 units each month:

margin of safety = 500 – 400 = 100 units

A negative margin of safety means the business is making losses.

Question

From data, calculate the breakeven level of output and margin of safety and interpret the result. Make decisions about how the firm should behave in the light of the breakeven value and the given situation.

Analysis In order to investigate how changes in price and cost affect a firm's profits, decision-makers can use the breakeven model. This is because it is a relatively straightforward tool to use and understand. It can also be used to see how sensitive profits are to changes in output levels.

Evaluation The usefulness of breakeven as a decision tool is limited where firms make more than one product. This is because the breakeven level of output for a product will change with a different allocation of fixed costs to that product.

Link Because one aspect of a price decision is the cost of manufacture, this section about costing has links to marketing, and in particular differentiated pricing.

Investment decisions

What is investment?

An investment is the expenditure of capital today in the expectation of future benefits. For the investment to be attractive, the future benefits must be of greater value than the required capital outlay. Hence, an investment decision is character-ised by:

- an initial capital outflow
- a series of future inflows

Inflows are given a positive sign, whereas payments (outflows) are identified as negatives.

Investment returns

A firm might invest £10,000 in a new machine that is expected to give future benefits of:

Year 1	£3,000
Year 2	£4,000
Year 3	£3,000
Year 4	£2,000

Investments are required to increase output or to maintain output if worn out assets need to be replaced. Investments can be made in assets, e.g. buying a new machine, or in people, e.g. employee training.

There are two investment decision methods required by the specification — the payback period and the accounting rate of return — and these are looked at below.

Payback period (PBP)

The PBP is the length of time taken for the sum of the inflows to match the initial investment exactly. It is calculated by adding the cumulative inflows until this value exactly equals the outflow. So, using the data from the above example:

	Flow (£)	Cumulative flow (£)
Year 0	−10,000	−10,000
Year 1	+3,000	−7,000
Year 2	+4,000	−3,000
Year 3	+3,000	0
Year 4	+2,000	+2,000

So, it takes 3 years for the initial investment to be paid back.

The PBP decision rule

The shorter the time required to achieve payback, the more attractive the investment. If a decision-maker is comparing two investments, then the one with the shorter PBP would be preferred. This is because the shorter the time until all of the capital has been recovered, the less risk there is of the anticipated inflows changing. Hence, PBP focuses upon risk reduction.

Accounting rate of return (ARR)

The ARR compares the average yearly profit from the investment to the amount of capital initially spent. The answer is expressed as a percentage, as this makes comparisons between different investments easier to evaluate. Using the above data:

	Flow (£)
Year 1	+3,000
Year 2	+4,000
Year 3	+3,000
Year 4	+2,000
Total	12,000
Outlay	−10,000
Total profit	£2,000

So, average profit $= \dfrac{\text{total profit}}{4} = \dfrac{£2,000}{4} = £500$

$\text{ARR} = \dfrac{\text{average profit}}{\text{investment}} \times 100 = \dfrac{£500}{£10,000} \times 100 = 5\%$

The ARR decision rule

The larger the percentage, the more attractive the investment. At a minimum, the ARR should exceed the opportunity cost of the capital. The cost of capital, in the absence of any other investments, would be bank interest rates. If a manager uses ARR, the objective is usually that of maximising profit. If a decision-maker is comparing two investments, then the one with the larger ARR would be preferred.

Question

From data, calculate PBP and ARR. Suggest whether the investment is appropriate in the light of the result of the calculation and the given situation.

Analysis The results of any investment calculation are only as good as the data supplied. Because investments are concerned with future events, it is not possible to be certain about the size and timing of the future cash flows. As such, a decision-maker would want to repeat the calculations using a different set of estimated inflows to see how sensitive the decision is to changed circumstances.

Evaluation Calculating both PBP and ARR might yield conflicting decisions. Whether an investment is attractive depends upon what the decision-maker is most concerned with: profit or risk reduction.

Link Because investments deal with future events, there are clear links with how changes in the firm's environment (see Unit 1) affect the anticipated inflows. Further, if the benefit of a training programme can be measured, then investment techniques can be used to assess whether training in employee skills was worthwhile (People in organisations).

Final accounts

Final accounts summarise a firm's position at the end of a period of time. Typically, this is annually, although they might be drawn up more frequently for managers. Final accounts are, therefore, historic. Consequently, for some users, final accounts are too old to be useful. The purpose of final accounts is to enable stakeholders to assess the position of the business.

Users of final accounts include owners, managers, employees, creditors, trade unions, potential investors and competitors.

Balance sheet

This is a summary of a business's assets and liabilities at a point in time. The main parts of a balance sheet are considered below.

Fixed assets
Items owned by the business which generate revenue, e.g. machinery, buildings.

Current assets
Items owned by the business that can be turned into cash in the next accounting period, e.g. stock, debtors.

Current liabilities
Debts which the business will have to pay back in the next accounting period, e.g. trade creditors.

Long-term liabilities
Debts which the business will have to pay back after the next accounting period, e.g. 5-year bank loan.

Owners' funds

Money invested in the business by the owners either as their initial investment or through the retained profits from previous years' trading.

The structure of a balance sheet

Business name and date		(£000s)
Fixed assets		200
Current assets	300	
Current liabilities	(180)	
Net current assets		120
ASSETS EMPLOYED		**320**
Financed by:		
Long-term liabilities		70
Owners' funds		250
CAPITAL EMPLOYED		**320**

Profit and loss account

The profit and loss account (P&L) is a summary of a business's revenues and costs for a period of time (usually 1 year). Profit is revenue minus costs.

The structure of a P&L account

Business name and date of period ending for the account	(£000s)
Revenue	1,120
Cost of goods sold	(820)
Gross profit	**300**
Expenses	(190)
Profit before interest and tax	**110**
Interest expense	(20)
Taxable profit	90
Taxation	(40)
Net profit	**50**

Net profit

Net profit is either distributed among the owners or retained in the business, typically for expansion purposes. The decision about what proportion of net profit is distributed to the owners rests with them. In companies where the owners are shareholders — and not necessarily directors or managers — the directors recommend the distribution of net profits, i.e. the dividend, and therefore the amount of retained profit. However, it is shareholders who make the decision at the annual general meeting (AGM) by voting to accept or reject this recommendation.

Question

From data, make amendments to a given set of final accounts. Suggest how final accounts could be used by stakeholders to make decisions regarding the future direction of the business.

Auditors

Company final accounts have to be checked by an auditor, whose role is to ensure that the accounts give a 'true and fair view' of the financial activities and position of the firm. By having the accounts verified by an independent outsider, the owners should be reassured that the information being given to them by the managers who are running their business is a true reflection of the state of that business.

An auditor's check of the final accounts reflects what has happened, rather than suggesting what the business might do in the future. As such, final accounts do not offer any guarantee that the business will continue to trade profitably in the future. It is therefore entirely possible for a business to have its accounts drawn up to the satisfaction of an auditor, yet fail soon after.

Links Only incorporated businesses — private and public limited companies — are legally required to publish final accounts (see Unit 1). Final accounts will be of interest to a wide range of stakeholders (see Unit 1) who will each have their own objectives in inspecting them.

Evaluation Final accounts only summarise items with a known financial value, e.g. the business's cash balance. There are many aspects to a successful business that would not appear within the final accounts, e.g. a good reputation within the market. Further, the level of detail in final accounts may not be sufficient for the particular needs of some stakeholders.

People in organisations

Parts of the human resources area of the specification do not readily lend themselves to assessment through short data–response questions. However, it is possible to assess some aspects of the human resources area, and these are identified here.

Human resource planning

Workforce planning

Workforce planning aims to ensure that the business has the quantity and quality of skills to meet its objectives.

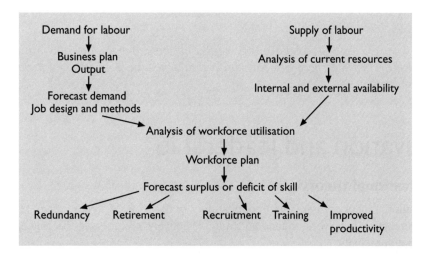

Question

From data, calculate the demand for labour for a particular level of output. Suggest how the firm might use workforce planning to ensure it has an appropriate supply of labour to enable it to meet its objectives and the decisions it would need to take in matching supply with demand.

Labour turnover

Labour turnover is calculated as:

$$\frac{\text{number of severances in a period}}{\text{average number of employees for the period}} \times 100\%$$

In any business, a degree of labour turnover is inevitable as people leave the business due to resignation, promotion elsewhere or retirement. Indeed, some labour turnover is advantageous as new recruits may bring in new ideas and enthusiasms. Further, people leaving senior posts provide internal promotion opportunities for those who remain. However, excessive labour turnover is potentially damaging, and increasing labour turnover could be a symptom of a demotivated workforce.

Implications of high labour turnover

Possible implications of high levels of labour turnover include:

- low employee morale
- absence of team feeling amongst a constantly changing workforce
- increased recruitment and selection costs
- increased training costs
- interruptions to production
- loss of quality
- poor reputation amongst potential recruits

Motivation and leadership

Motivational theory

Motivational theory requires an understanding of the work of Taylor, Mayo, Maslow and Herzberg. Their work, individually and collectively, gives rise to the concepts of:

- job enlargement
- job enrichment
- job rotation
- team working
- employee participation
- delegation
- employee empowerment

Monetary and non-monetary motivation

Motivation includes monetary and non-monetary motivation. Monetary motivation assumes that employees will change their work habits if offered sufficient financial gain. This view is compatible with the work of Taylor and linked to Maslow's lower order needs. A bonus, or other incentive scheme, will only be effective if:

- the link between performance and the incentive is understood by employees
- employees trust managers to pay the bonus
- employees feel the bonus has value

To be effective, the payment of bonuses must increase the value of output by more than the cost of the scheme.

Low motivation

Low levels of motivation in an organisation lead to:

- low levels of output
- low levels of quality
- an increased number of accidents

- high levels of absenteeism
- high levels of labour turnover

Leadership

Leadership describes the ability to influence the behaviour of another. This ability stems from the power a person can exercise. The source of this power might be due to their personality or some other personal trait, their position within an organisation, their ability to reward or punish, or their knowledge.

Leadership styles

Three leadership styles are identified:

- autocratic
- democratic
- laissez-faire

Whether a particular leadership style is appropriate will depend on:

- the situation, i.e. whether it is familiar, complex, routine, etc.
- the maturity of the followers in terms of their willingness and ability
- the abilities and values of the leader

> **Links** Much of operations management is concerned with the coordination and arrangement of employees so as to enable them to produce a product. There are links with motivation and leadership (People in organisations). In particular, a culture of teamwork and participation relies heavily on the way in which employees are led.

Management structure and design

The specification identifies two concepts: span of control and hierarchy.

Span of control

This is the number of followers (i.e. employees) who report directly to a leader. There is no ideal span of control for all situations. The appropriate span of control reflects:

- the ability of the leader
- the abilities and motivation of the followers
- the complexity of the task

Too narrow a span of control can:

- stifle follower initiative through intensive supervision
- reduce possibilities for delegation and employee development
- create a structure with many layers that might hinder communication

Too wide a span of control can lead to:

- inadequate levels of supervision

- followers feeling alienated and remote
- few opportunities for follower advancement
- excessive leader workloads

Hierarchy

This describes the number of layers within an organisational structure. The more layers there are, the greater the distance messages have to travel to get to their intended recipient. This may distort and slow communication and decision-making.

Operations management

Operations management is concerned with the process that converts scarce resources into sellable outputs for the satisfaction of customers' needs. All businesses engage in this process, although it is often easier to visualise this in the context of a manufacturing organisation.

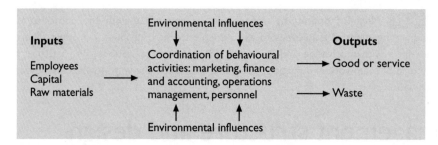

An efficient business is one that can produce the desired level of sellable output with the lowest level of waste, using the minimum amount of inputs.

Operational efficiency

Scale

Scale describes the size of a business. Size can be measured in several ways:
- legal structure, e.g. sole trader versus plc
- financial measures, e.g. assets, profits, market capitalisation
- number of employees
- market share, i.e. company sales ÷ total sales
- concentration ratio, i.e. sales of x top firms ÷ total sales
- Companies Act, 1985

Link Go to Unit 1.

Increased size

Increased size can be achieved by:

- internal, organic growth
- external, acquisitive growth

Increases in size make a firm more dominant in the market and more able to set price and supply rather than having to respond to them. But the process of growth can lead to problems. These include:

- integrating two cultures if growth is through acquisition
- loss of management focus on the business's main activity
- increased workloads
- reduced morale amongst employees feeling insecure in their role

Capacity utilisation

At any given size, the business can operate at its capacity, which is its notional potential maximum output. The closer the business operates to this level in any given period of time, the higher its capacity utilisation. This is measured as:

$$\text{capacity utilisation} = \frac{\text{output}}{\text{potential output}} \times 100\%$$

A firm operating at 100% capacity utilisation is using all of its inputs to their maximum. This may be desirable in the short term but could be potentially damaging in the longer term, unless allowance is made for worker fatigue and maintenance of capital equipment within the calculation of potential output. A firm operating at 0% capacity utilisation is, by definition, not producing. However, it will still be incurring fixed costs and so will be making losses. Consequently, firms will seek to operate as close to their capacity as is sustainable, by balancing the benefits against the costs associated with high levels of utilisation.

Firms can operate above capacity for short periods of time by:

- overtime working
- rescheduling maintenance
- acquiring the temporary use of capacity, e.g. leasing an additional machine

Question
From data, calculate the capacity utilisation for a business. Suggest how the business could optimise its utilisation and discuss decisions that would need to be taken to ensure this is achieved.

Changing levels of output

When output levels fluctuate, firms have problems in securing an appropriate supply of inputs, including employees, raw material, machinery, storage and working capital.

Operating at a steady output presents fewer problems. Businesses can maintain consistent output by using stocks to separate the business from its immediate environment. For example, when capacity exceeds demand, excess finished goods are held in storage; these can be sold later when demand exceeds capacity.

Evaluation The business would need to assess whether the benefits of a steady level of output outweigh the additional cost penalties of holding stock.

Question
From data, calculate the average output required for a period of time. Suggest how the firm might optimise the utilisation of its capacity to meet the demand facing it.

Under-usage of capacity
The effects of under-utilisation of capacity are not all negative. Consequently, managers may deliberately decide to operate at less than 100% capacity utilisation. The implications of this choice include:
- increased cost per unit (fixed cost spread across fewer units)
- reduced profits due to cost penalties
- failure to supply the market if demand exceeds current output
- customer frustration due to shortages of supply
- difficulties in re-establishing links with suppliers when demand increases
- boredom amongst employees
- falling employee morale due to fears of long-term security of employment, with possible loss of key staff
- lower fatigue amongst staff, with reduced absenteeism
- reduced risk of accidents
- opportunities to engage in unscheduled equipment maintenance
- reduction in cash outflows as payments for total variable costs fall

Increasing capacity
Increased utilisation requires either an increase in output or a reduction in capacity, or a combination of both. Some methods of reducing capacity are short run and suitable for temporary reduction, e.g. reduced hours. Other methods have a longer-term implication, e.g. closure of a facility. Possible means of increasing utilisation include:
- a marketing campaign to stimulate market demand
- better maintenance to reduce breakdowns
- employee training to increase efficiency
- holding more stocks to insulate the firm from external shocks
- disposal of permanently redundant capacity
- short time working

Question

From data, determine the level of capacity utilisation. Discuss whether this level might be a deliberate choice and consider its short and longer-term implications.

Economies of scale

Economies of scale describe the long-run fall in unit cost as output increases. They can be either internal, i.e. they apply to the single firm, or external, i.e. they apply to the whole industry.

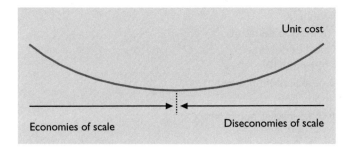

Internal economies of scale
Examples of internal economies of scale are:
- purchasing — bulk buying reduces unit cost
- technical — larger output enables the use of more efficient techniques
- financial — improved access to capital because of reduced creditor risk

External economies of scale
Examples of external economies of scale are:
- improvements in infrastructure, e.g. communication links
- suppliers locating close to major market
- skilled pool of labour, e.g. local colleges providing industry-specific training

Diseconomies of scale
Diseconomies of scale describe the rise in unit cost as output rises: hence as output continues to rise, the business suffers a unit cost penalty. Examples of diseconomies of scale centre on human factors, and consequently there are clear links with motivation and leadership. Examples of reasons for diseconomies of scale are:
- loss of control by managers
- remoteness of managers
- inefficient communication due to layers of hierarchy
- inter-departmental rivalry and a breakdown of coordination
- employee alienation and a lack of team feeling leading to labour turnover
- inflexibility in systems and increased bureaucracy

Organising production

Operations management is concerned with converting scarce resources into sellable outputs. The way in which this transformational process is organised reflects several factors, which include:

- variability of market demand
- volume of market demand
- uniformity of product
- availability of skilled employees
- employee motivation
- availability of specialist machinery

Types of production

The main types of production are job, batch, flow, cell and lean production.

Job production

The approach of providing one-off products which have high levels of variability.

Batch production

The division of production into self-contained stages, each being completed before the commencement of the next stage.

Flow production

Also known as mass production, this is the sub-division of labour with high levels of specialisation and repetition.

A firm faced with high degrees of variability of demand in a relatively low volume market may employ job production, e.g. civil engineering. In contrast, a firm facing consistently high volumes of demand for an essentially uniform product may employ flow production, e.g. safety pins.

Cell and lean production

These approaches to production are about management and leadership rather than the physical manufacturing process. Hence, it is possible to adopt lean techniques within a job environment, a cell approach with a flow environment etc.

Cell production is characterised by:
- self-contained units of employees and machinery, i.e. cells
- high levels of employee empowerment
- self-responsibility for quality
- production of significant proportions of the total product, or the entire product
- a culture of teamwork

Lean production is characterised by:
- elimination of waste at all stages in the process
- responsiveness to changes in market demand
- flexibility
- production initiated by customer order
- focus on quality and the 'right first time' approach
- integration of development and manufacturing
- employee responsibility and involvement in decisions

> **Link** Both cell and lean production emphasise the role of the employee. Consequently, there are clear links with motivation and leadership. Although many employees may welcome the additional responsibility arising from the lean approach, some may not. Therefore, the adoption of a new method of organising production will require careful attention to the management of the process of change. Further links are between lean production and marketing (product development), stock control (just-in-time, JIT), and quality (total quality management, TQM).

Quality

Customers may be internal, i.e. the next stage in the process, or external, i.e. the person who buys the item from the firm. Quality is important because it leads to customer satisfaction.

Inadequate quality leads to reduced profits due to:
- poor reputation and lack of repeat purchases by the customer
- the costs of reworking faulty items
- the costs of scrapping items
- the costs of replacing defective items
- the administration costs of guarantees and customer returns
- the legal costs in defending the company against customers' legal actions

The main approaches to quality are:
- quality assurance
- total quality management
- benchmarking

Quality assurance

Quality assurance means ensuring every item conforms to specification. This can be achieved through built-in quality or by checking quality.

Built-in quality

Built-in quality means ensuring that every part of the process conforms to requirements. Quality is considered during product design, process design, materials procurement etc. Once an item has been subject to a process, the employee who undertakes that process ensures it complies with the requirement before it moves to the next stage. This necessitates that the employee:
- is fully trained
- is equipped with the ability to assess the output
- has something meaningful to assess
- has the authority to intervene if a process is producing outside specifications

In this way, by making the item correctly at every stage, the final product will emerge with zero defects. Benefits of built-in quality include:
- consistent quality
- higher levels of employee motivation through job enrichment
- reduced cost
- fewer defects, waste and rework
- a culture where quality is seen as an intrinsic part of the job

Checking quality

Checking quality means inspecting items to ensure compliance with requirements. It is typically conducted by a team of quality assurance inspectors. Benefits include:
- a reduced need for training
- a greater likelihood that defects will be spotted and remedial action taken

Disadvantages of the checking quality approach include the following:
- quality is seen as being separate from the process
- defects are only apparent after the process
- a divisive culture may emerge, quality being someone else's responsibility
- unless every item is inspected, poor quality may still reach the customer

Question
From data, determine the costs of poor quality and its possible causes, and discuss appropriate decisions and actions to ensure improvements in quality. Discuss the implications of methods of improving quality for customers, employees and managers.

Total quality management

Total quality management (TQM) is a management approach where all see a quality culture as of vital importance and as their responsibility. It puts customer satisfaction at the heart of every process, whether the customer is internal or the final, external customer.

> **Evaluation/Links** For TQM to take root, employees have to be trained in quality issues and managers have to value employee input. Further, quality has to be seen to matter. If there is a gap between what managers say and what they accept, then attempts to adopt TQM will fail. A TQM culture requires an open style of management and so may not flourish in structures described by McGregor's Theory X or the views of Taylor.

Benchmarking

Benchmarking is comparison with the best. It is not copying. It means learning from the best and adapting ideas and techniques to the particular set of circumstances within the business. It involves:
- identifying an area or part of a process that is to be benchmarked
- measuring performance prior to benchmarking
- setting a target for improvement
- investigating the processes of the firm which is acting as the benchmark
- adapting the process to the situation within the firm
- measuring performance after benchmarking

Stock control

The purpose of stock is to act as a buffer between different stages of a chain, whether internally between different stages of production, or externally between the firm and its suppliers/customers. The role of stock is to decouple supply and demand. Stock can be:
- raw materials — items awaiting the beginning of a production process
- work in progress — items within the transformational process
- finished goods — completed items awaiting sale to a customer

Holding stock

Holding stock allows a firm to:
- produce if its supplier fails to deliver
- produce if a machine breaks down
- sell if its production process comes to a halt

Cost of holding stock
This costs money because:
- it ties up capital in acquiring the stock
- it ties up cash in paying for processing
- it requires storage, so leading to costs such as insurance and heating

- every time the stock is moved, handling costs are incurred
- materials may perish or become obsolete

Cost of not holding stock

This means the firm:
- cannot gain economies of scale
- cannot take cost advantages of uninterrupted production runs
- runs the risk of not being able to supply
- cannot benefit from speculative gains

Implications of stock holding

The amount of stock held will reflect the:
- nature of the good, e.g. supermarkets hold low levels of stock of perishable goods
- market being served, e.g. Christmas crackers are seasonal
- production process, e.g. a chemical plant will need adequate supplies of raw materials to maintain continuous production

Other stock control considerations

Buffer stocks

Buffer stocks are the minimum amount of stock held by a firm. Stock levels should not fall below this amount. They are held to act as an insurance against interruption in supply or sudden increases in demand.

Reorder level

The reorder level is the amount of stock that triggers the acquisition of a new delivery. It will reflect the reliability of the supplier and the rate of usage.

Lead-time

The lead-time is the period between placing an order and the availability of stock to the production process.

Questions

From stock usage and delivery data, determine:
- *an appropriate buffer stock*
- *an appropriate reorder level*
- *an appropriate lead-time*

Suggest how the firm could decide each of these.

Stock control charts

A stock control chart is a graphic depiction of stock usage and deliveries over a period of time. It combines the three stock-holding concepts outlined above. In the chart, the steeper the gradient of the lines, the greater the rate of stock usage.

Stock control chart

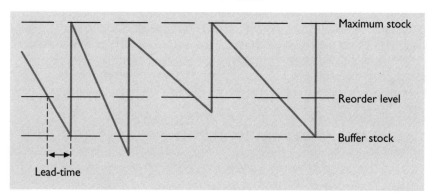

- Maximum stock
- Reorder level
- Buffer stock

Lead-time

> **Question**
>
> From stock usage and delivery data, construct a stock control chart. Alternatively, interpret usage, lead-time, buffer stock and reorder level from a given stock chart. Suggest how improvements could be made in the stock position of the firm.

Just–in–time production

In a situation where there is no variation in demand and no variation in supply, a firm would not need to hold contingency stocks. This situation is termed just-in-time (JIT) and is an approach to manufacturing and stock holding in which excess stock is eliminated throughout the process. The consequences of operating a JIT system include:

- reduced stock-holding costs
- increased unit acquisition cost (no purchasing economies of scale)
- quicker response to changes in customer demand (no stocks of raw materials)
- improvements in quality
- vulnerability of processing to breakdowns in the supply of materials
- vulnerability of sales to stoppages in the production process
- the exposure of weaknesses in communication channels, either within the firm or between the firm and its suppliers and customers

> **Question**
>
> From stock data, determine whether JIT is a suitable approach. Suggest what conditions might need to be established so that JIT could be adopted.

Questions
&
Answers

In this section we consider three original data–response examination papers, each of which has two questions. These have been written to reflect the style used by the examination board in terms of source, length, vocabulary and complexity.

This section provides learning opportunities in two ways. First, the mock examination papers can be used for revision practice. Each is typical of the examination that you will face and as such they make excellent revision material. They should be answered in the 75 minutes allowed for the examination.

The second way in which this section can help maximise your grade is through an analysis of the work of two students. Each answer is accompanied by a detailed commentary from an experienced examiner. This commentary is identified by the icon *e*. The critique discusses the good and weak points within the students' work. Where there are weaknesses, suggestions for improvement are given. By carefully reading both the answers and the examiner's comments, you will see how more of the available marks can be gained.

Having answered the questions yourself, compare your responses with the answers from the two students. By benchmarking your performance, you will be able to make improvements.

Question 1

Marketing a luxury hotel

Over the last few years, Hutton Hall hotel has been seeking to promote itself as an ideal venue for luxurious breaks, away from the pressures of a busy life. The hotel's general manager, Pauline Mills, has recently received a report from a firm of marketing consultants. To collect the data, the consultants conducted face-to-face interviews asking the opinions of 100 guests (who formed a stratified quota sample). Each guest was asked a number of structured questions to give the hotel a score on a scale of 1 (unacceptable) to 9 (excellent). The results are shown in Table 1.

Table 1 Results of interviews with Hutton Hall hotel guests

Feature	Minimum	Mean	Maximum
Cleanliness	2	6.8	9
Staff attitude	2	5.6	8
Food	1	7.2	9
Facilities	3	6.1	9
Value for money	3	6.9	9

Pauline hopes to use the report to construct a marketing plan for the hotel for the next 6 months. Her annual marketing budget is £40,000, half of which could be spent on magazine advertising. She is keen to ensure that she communicates with the market segment she is targeting through the most appropriate message. The data in Table 2 will help her decide how she might achieve a cost-effective way of doing this.

Table 2 Monthly advertising rates and market segment

Magazine	Circulation	Cost per ½ page	Reader profile (socio-economic group)
A	54,000	£1,500	A, B and C1
B	60,000	£1,350	B and C1
C	38,000	£2,000	A and B
D	80,000	£1,750	B, C1 and C2

(a) Outline the reasons for having a target market segment. (4 marks)

(b) Explain the data collection method used by the consultants. (6 marks)

(c) Refer to Table 2. Assuming that Pauline does not wish to target C2s, calculate which magazine is the most cost effective for advertising. (4 marks)

(d) Suggest a suitable marketing plan for the Hutton Hall hotel. (15 marks)

Total: 29 marks

Answer to paper 1, question 1: candidate A

(a) The reasons for having a target market are so that Hutton Hall know who to direct their advertising at, i.e. top market segment — advertise in society magazines. They will not want to waste their £40,000 budget on something that will not be directed towards the correct group. It states that they would like to market themselves as a luxurious break, away from the pressures of a busy life. So Hutton Hall should target businessmen and women by advertising in the business sections of newspapers and magazines.

> This is a good answer which clearly demonstrates an understanding of the concept of a target market. The candidate usefully suggests that the target market is the customers with whom the business wants to communicate: this avoids the risk of wasting budgetary expenditure on people who would not be interested in the hotel's offering. The suggestion that the target market might be businessmen and women exemplifies the concept of a distinct group. This answer demonstrates the candidate's ability to apply knowledge to the situation and, as such, it is application at L2 and would gain full marks.

(b) The consultants used the method of asking 100 guests 5 questions about the hotel. They then took a mean for the categories, revealing that Hutton Hall was average on everything and some way below the luxurious hotel they were trying to portray.

> The candidate has described the methods used rather than explaining them. Further, the candidate has merely repeated the terms used without any real attempt to demonstrate what they are. As such, at best the answer shows an appreciation of the vocabulary of the subject rather than understanding of it. Consequently, it could not be rewarded as application at L2 and so would gain less than half of the available marks.
>
> It is entirely possible that the candidate could offer an explanation if encouraged, but the examiner cannot do this. Remember, you will be assessed by what you write down and not what you could have written. Consequently, it is vital that your answers are as full as possible.

(c) Magazine A = £1,500 ÷ 54,000 = £0.0278
Magazine B = £1,350 ÷ 60,000 = £0.0225
Magazine C = £2,000 ÷ 38,000 = £0.0526
Magazine D = £1,750 ÷ 80,000 = £0.0219

Magazine D is the cheapest per reader and so that is the one Pauline should use.

> The candidate has not read the question with sufficient care and has penalised herself as a consequence. Careful reading of the question shows that Pauline does not want to target C2s and, as such, magazine D is not suitable for her target market. Hence, the calculation of the cost per reader need not be performed for this magazine. However, there is no penalty other than the time used because examiners do not mark negatively. But the answer does illustrate the need to be

diligent in carefully reading the question so as not to waste valuable examination time. Another point worth noting is that answers to calculations are not always convenient round numbers.

The calculations for the other magazines are correct, as is the conclusion given the evidence the candidate has available. The candidate would get 3 marks.

(d) A suitable marketing plan would be to advertise in business magazines, as they reach the type of clients they require in order to market their hotel as a luxurious break away. They could offer their hotel as a conference centre so the business people can see what Hutton has to offer. This in turn will make them want to come back in their own leisure time.

🖉 This answer is far too brief given the question's requirement and the mark allocation. Further, it can be argued that it fails to offer a marketing plan. Instead, the answer offers some elements of the marketing mix, which is not the same thing. The elements offered are advertising (promotion) and a conference centre (product). The fact that there is some attempt to link these two ideas to Pauline's target market just lifts the answer into application at L2.

■ ■ ■

Answer to paper 1, question 1: candidate B

(a) It enables them to channel their money into the appropriate advertising media, thus saving money by spending only where it is going to be seen and noticed by the target group.

Market segmentation enables them to aim at the type of people that would be interested in the services of Hutton Hall. Pauline is then able to optimise the costs of any communication she tries to make in the future, by being more aware that they may well have a genuine interest in the hotel and that her efforts may be more productive as opposed to being wasted on people who may not be able to afford the services, too young or too old to use the services and other such people who would like to have an interest in the hotel.

🖉 This has elements of both a good answer and a weak answer. It is good in that the candidate clearly understands the concept of target marketing. The main points the examiner could expect are in the answer and the examples serve to reinforce the ideas the candidate puts forward. The examples also serve to contextualise the answer.

The first weakness is that the expression, or quality of written communication, is poor: the last sentence is far too complex and too long. Never forget the merit of short, crisp sentences. The second weakness is that the answer is simply too long. The key word in the question is 'outline'; add this to the mark allocation and this should suggest to the candidate that a brief answer would be sufficient. Although there is nothing in the content which detracts from the quality of the answer, the worry would be that the candidate will run out of time towards the end of the examination. This means that the candidate will not give enough time and attention to the final, major question. Avoid the ever-present temptation to write too much for the first answer.

However, because the answer demonstrates application of knowledge to the situation, full marks would be awarded at the top level (L2) here.

(b) The sampling was conducted in a face-to-face manner. This may have deterred the guests from being brutally honest, making them give ratings which might be slightly higher so as not to appear rude. The results may therefore be biased and untrue, which is something that needs to be taken into consideration before any large amount of money is spent as a result of the market research. I notice that there was only one rating of 1, unacceptable. This makes me think people were not being honest because, among 100 people, some people are almost bound to think badly of the hotel. The people chosen formed a stratified quota sample, which means that the type of guests the hotel has is divided up into groups, and a set number are asked questions from each group. This method of sampling helps to ensure that the questioner doesn't just ask one type of person but asks all of the sorts of people that go to the hotel, so the sample properly reflects the guests. As the people who they asked are already guests in the hotel they must already like it or they wouldn't have gone there in the first place. Pauline Mills may consider asking people who may be in her target group but haven't necessarily been there many times before to find out what their initial thoughts were.

This is a good answer that clearly demonstrates understanding of both the sampling methodology used and the context. The comments about the method in the middle of the answer show understanding of the sampling method used, and the candidate is able to explain why this method might have been chosen (to ensure the sample is a representative sub-set of the overall population from which it is drawn).

The consideration of the validity of the results is good and the reference to the data in Table 1 is pleasing as it shows that the candidate recognises the need to make use of the information presented in the question. The candidate also points out usefully that the results of the research might not be wholly reliable. Overall, this answer demonstrates a good application of this part of the specification and the majority of the marks are gained for application at L2.

(c) The cheapest magazine is B because it costs £0.0225 per reader.

This is another good response in that the candidate has the answer the examiner is expecting. Hence, all of the available marks would be awarded. However, the failure to show examination method is both very poor technique and very high risk. If the candidate had written down the value incorrectly, then the answer would have received no credit. It is important that the various steps are shown in calculations, so that even if an error is made, subsequent marks for the rest of the answer can be gained.

(d) A marketing plan is the way in which the elements of the marketing mix are put together to reach the objective set by the business. The first thing that Pauline needs to do is to set herself an aim so that she, and others, know what they are hoping to do which is to move the hotel more up-market. Pauline has been sensible in first carrying out some research to find out what her customers think of the hotel and now she is able to make the necessary changes. However, as I said in my last answer, I don't think she should trust the answers she has. From the answers it is clear that one thing they need to do is to improve the staff attitude as this gets the lowest score. Maybe she needs to talk to whoever does the training, so that staff know how to treat guests. There is no point in attracting people to a luxury hotel if they aren't treated well because they will just feel conned, having paid a lot of money but got poor service. Pauline Mills may think about advertising in magazines such as *Tatler* and *Harpers & Queen*. These are aimed at busy city, fashion-conscious people who could afford such luxurious breaks. They may also consider advertising in a Sunday newspaper such as *The Times* when busy business people have time to read and consider how much they need a break and the pros and cons of doing so, which they may not do in the rush of a week day. She may think about offering facilities which may appeal to a businessman such as corporate rooms. Price will also be very important because if it is too low people won't believe the adverts about it being a luxury because people expect to have to pay a lot for a luxury. But if the price is high then the hotel has to be very good otherwise people won't come back and it is harder to attract people than to get them to return.

The candidate's answer starts off well with a clear definition of a marketing plan. This start should have then provided the structure of the rest of the answer. It is therefore disappointing that the remainder of the response does not have greater form. There could have been a paragraph on each of the elements, with a final concluding paragraph to bring the whole answer together.

The candidate's journey through the elements of the marketing mix is sound. By pointing to the linkages between the elements, for example between high price and luxury product, the candidate demonstrates awareness that marketing is an integrative function. This lifts the answer from a series of independent visits to each of the 4Ps in the marketing mix and gives the answer some suggestion of a strategy. The overall mark is within L3, analysis, with this higher skill being most evident in the final two sentences.

■ ■ ■

Question 2

Assessing a training scheme

Basit Nasim is a training manager at Fullbright Engineering Ltd. The production workers are organised into shopfloor teams and each team has a supervisor who is responsible for all aspects of its performance. Teams are eligible for a monthly bonus if their collective performance achieves a set amount of sellable output: scrap items cannot be sold. New team members undergo on-the-job training so that they can do any of the five tasks required.

Basit has just spent £7,000 of the company's money training one of the teams and he is now anxious to assess whether the structured off-the-job course was beneficial. To decide whether the course was worthwhile, Basit knew he would need to show the production manager some evidence. Consequently, Basit secretly measured the team's performance for 2 weeks before the training. After the 1-week course, he asked the supervisor to measure the team for another 2 weeks. Basit has calculated weekly averages for four criteria. These calculations are shown in Table 1.

Table 1 Training scheme schedule

Week	Production (000s)	Scrap (%)	Accidents	Absenteeism
1	18.0	8.0	0	1
2	17.8	8.0	0	2
3	Training			
4	19.2	4.6	1	0
5	19.2	4.4	0	0

Fullbright Engineering sells the part that the team produces for £0.25. If he can gain the support of the production manager, Basit hopes to extend the training scheme to all production workers.

(a) Explain the term on-the-job training. (4 marks)
(b) Calculate the monetary value of the mean weekly improvement in sellable output. (6 marks)
(c) Calculate the payback period for the training scheme. (4 marks)
(d) Discuss whether the training scheme should be extended to all production workers. (15 marks)

Total: 29 marks

■ ■ ■

Answer to paper 1, question 2: candidate A

(a) On-the-job training is undertaken whilst under normal working conditions. It is sometimes called sitting next to Nellie which means someone shows you how to do the job whilst they are working and then gives you a go whilst they watch you to see you do it right. This is a cheap way of training but it does mean people's bad habits can be passed on.

> This is a good answer in the context of the trigger word in the question, 'explain', and the mark allocation. The candidate clearly understands the meaning of on-the-job training and is able to give an advantage and a disadvantage of this method. The answer would be rewarded as application at L2, which is all that is required.

(b) Before training, output average: $\dfrac{18,000 + 17,800}{2} = 17,900$ units

Scrap is 8% so they can sell: $17,900 \times \dfrac{92}{100} = 16,468$

0.25p each is £4,117

After training, output average: 19,200 with 4.5% scrap

So they can sell: $19,200 \times \dfrac{95.5}{100} = 18,336$

0.25p each is £4,584

Improvement of £467

> This answer is good and gains maximum marks because the candidate has achieved the expected value. In terms of examination method, it is sensible that the candidate has labelled each of the stages gone through so that it is possible for the examiner to follow the approach. This approach could have been more efficient had the candidate determined the difference in output first, and then converted this into a monetary value: this saves a repeated calculation and thus some time. Top marks here, well deserved.

(c) Payback period = cost/saving
So payback is 7,000/467 = 14.99 weeks = 15 weeks.

> Full marks for this answer as it is correct. Again, the candidate's technique is good in that a formula is offered before values are put down.

(d) I think that the training scheme should be extended to everyone as the test group has shown that training can produce significant improvements. Waste can almost be halved from 8% down to about 4.5% and over 1 year the extra turnover for just one group continues to be significant after the payback period. In the 2 weeks after training, absenteeism was zero compared to 1 and 2 in weeks 1 and 2 respectively. Before finally commencing training for everyone I would recommend the supervisor continues to monitor the trained group for a much more extended period. This would enable Fullbright to assess fully the benefits of training —

2 weeks is not a very good time to assess, as the team's productivity may have been affected by the fact that they had just been away from work for a week and might feel rested. If, after this extended period of monitoring, it was shown that such production, scrap rates and absenteeism figures mirrored those of weeks 4 and 5 then I would strongly recommend that all employees undertake the training. However, if the accident figures remained above those of the pre-training period, then the situation should be reviewed (preferably via safety review as opposed to a training viability review).

> *②* After having told the reader her view, the candidate goes on to offer clear balance in the answer by considering a number of valid viewpoints. Throughout the answer, the candidate is weighing up the arguments both for and against extending the training. An example of this is the discussion regarding the short period of time over which the improvement has been seen. The fact that another non-training explanation might be the possible reason for the improvement is a good point. In this way, the candidate is able to offer a reasoned approach and thoroughly deserves to gain access to the highest level in the mark scheme.

■ ■ ■

Answer to paper 1, question 2: candidate B

(a) On-the-job training is when new employees will be on the shop floor observing and perhaps being involved in the work. The other way is off-the-job training which is when the person is sent away on a course or to college to learn new skills. This is the best way because the person can have lots of goes at doing the job and it doesn't really matter if they get it wrong because what they make isn't going to be sold. Another good thing is that it doesn't hold anyone up.

> *②* The candidate has answered a different question from the one that was actually asked. With the exception of the first sentence, the answer is not about 'on-the-job training' and so it is not relevant. This is a pity because much of what the candidate writes is sound. The first sentence is enough for the candidate to gain marks for demonstrating knowledge of on-the-job training.

(b) 17,900 × 25p = £4,475
19,200 × 25p = £4,800
So improvement = £325 each week

> *②* The answer contains a number of weaknesses. First, and most obviously, the candidate has not recognised the improvement in scrap rates. Rather, she has focused purely on the increase in output. It is left to the examiner to recognise that **17,900** is the average output before the training. The second weakness is the absence of any indication of what the numbers on the page actually are. It is important that method is clearly set out so that the examiners can follow your approach, especially if it is different from the one they might have been expecting. Overall, this answer gets only half marks.

(c) Payback period is 21.5 weeks.

ⓔ Given the error in answering the previous question, it is entirely reasonable that the candidate has given this answer. As this correctly follows on from part (b), the examiner can give full marks under the 'own figure rule'. But again note the poor method. Indeed, if the candidate had written the answer on the mark scheme, 15 weeks, then no marks would have been awarded as this is inconsistent with the weekly improvement answer. However, had the candidate at least written the formula, then she would have got 1 of the 4 marks. So, remember, always show method.

(d) Perhaps it should be extended, as the signs are good. Not only does the production increase by over 1,000 units but the percentage of scrap has decreased to an average of 4.5%. But the workers have only just been trained and possibly are keen to impress and so work harder, especially as they know they are being watched by their supervisor. But as the months go by, possibly the work group won't have such enthusiasm and so their output may fall back closer to what it was before the training week. It is a lot of money to spend on a production team, though it does depend on how many workers are in the whole production team. The case says that each worker can do any of the five tasks, so maybe there are five workers. If so, it costs more than £1,000 to train each worker, which is a lot. The absenteeism figures are pretty pointless as the figures are only one or two. Another thing is that the extra output might be due to the fall in absenteeism because they know the supervisor is watching them and not because of the training. If so, when the supervisor stops looking so closely, the absenteeism might go back up again and the output would fall. Perhaps this is rather like the Hawthorne experiments by Elton Mayo. The workforce may be reacting to the increased supervision by working harder. Possibly the firm should be looking to other methods, less costly ones such as a greater focus on production workers and manager relations. Another reason for the training is that it might be good for the workers as Herzberg says that training is a motivator. This might be why the absenteeism has fallen after the course. Motivated workers are important for the business since quality improves as well, as they take more care of what they are doing. But one risk is that the workers might want to be paid more or, worse, they might leave and get another job somewhere else because they have better skills than before. But provided they stay on for more than 22 weeks, the business doesn't lose any money.

ⓔ This is a very good answer. It is also longer than one might expect: perhaps not showing the method for the calculations enabled the candidate to save some time which was used on this last question. The discussion considers both sides of the argument and suggests how the improvements might have come about. The integration of human resources management (HRM) theory and the impact of training on motivation and quality is good and demonstrates the candidate's ability to see the issue as being multifaceted. The one major disappointment is that the candidate does not actually come to a final view. However, given the wording of the question, this is not strictly required and as such it is quite legitimate. As the answer is evaluative, the candidate would gain the majority of the marks.

✍ **Candidate A scored more highly on the questions about Fullbright than the questions about Hutton Hall. Despite the good answers to the Fullbright questions, which were of A-grade standard, the candidate's performance overall did not accumulate enough marks to be awarded a grade A. One possibility is that the subject matter of the first question, marketing, was not to the candidate's liking. Whatever the reason, it illustrates the importance of having a firm grasp of the entire specification, rather than just parts of it. Overall, a C grade would be awarded.**

Candidate B was more consistent, but missed a certain A grade by virtue of the poor handling of the quantitative questions. Another disappointment is the relatively poor quality of written communication in many of the answers, particularly with regard to the flow of sentences in the final part of Question 2. Consequently, the candidate failed to gain all of the marks for this aspect of the examination, such that her final grade would be on the borderline between A and B.

aper 2

Question 1

Deciding whether to accept an order

Luxe Ltd manufactures electric lights and has recently received an enquiry from a retailer that it does not currently supply. The retailer wants 6,000 units of a motion-sensitive security light. They are to be delivered in 3 months at a unit price of £7.50. The order is very similar to a current product, the MSL45, which Luxe already manufactures. However, accepting the order would mean spending £5,000 on a new machine tool to enable the existing machinery to make the new product as well as the MSL45. The normal operating capacity of the existing machinery is 2,000 MSL45s per week. Table 1 shows its planned usage for the next 8 weeks.

Table 1 Planned usage of MSL45 machine tool

Week	Planned output
1	2,000
2	2,000
3	1,800
4	1,500
5	1,000
6	1,000
7	800
8	800

The accounts department has the information about the MSL45 as shown in Table 2.

Table 2 Costs associated with operating the MSL45 machine tool

Variable cost per unit	
Labour	£2.50
Materials	£3.50
Fixed cost per unit	£2.00
Profit per unit	£0.50
Price	£8.50

(a) **Explain the term fixed cost per unit as used in Table 2.** (4 marks)

(b) **Calculate the total contribution of the new order.** (6 marks)

(c) **Outline suitable tactics, which could be used to produce temporarily more than the normal operating capacity of the machinery.** (4 marks)

(d) **Discuss whether the order should be accepted.** (15 marks)

Total: 29 marks

■ ■ ■

paper 2

Answer to paper 2, question 1: candidate A

(a) Fixed cost per unit is the cost to produce one unit. Fixed costs are the costs that do not change as a result of the level of output, e.g. rent, depreciation, taxes etc.

> 🖊 By confusing fixed costs and total costs, the candidate does not make the best of starts. However, the attempted definition of fixed cost, and its exemplification, is enough to demonstrate knowledge of this cost. Note, though, that the definition of fixed cost is weak in that it does not recognise that fixed costs do not vary with output in the short run. The examiners would reward the candidate at L1.

(b)
7.50 × 6,000	=	£45,000
Minus new tools	=	£4,000
40,000 − (8 × 6,000)	=	−8,000
−8,000 + (0.5 × 6,000)	=	−5,000
Total contribution	=	−£5,000

> 🖊 The answer given is not that expected and so full marks are not available. The presentation of the answer is poor and the examiner has to unravel what the candidate is really trying to do. The candidate is not helping the examiner. The assumption is that the first line relates to the revenue from the order. Similarly, the figure 8 in the third line appears to be the unit cost (£2.50 + £3.50 + £2.00). If this is indeed the case, then the inclusion of fixed costs suggests that the candidate does not understand the concept of contribution. An error is that the new tools have a cost of £5,000, not £4,000 as suggested by the candidate. Overall, it is not possible to reward this answer.

(c) The firm could try to persuade workers to work overtime. This means that they stay on after their normal hours and do a bit extra so the machines are working for more hours and they can make more parts. But the workers would get paid a higher rate and this would mean the cost of the parts would go up.

> 🖊 The candidate offers an appropriate method of boosting output for short periods of time. The fact that the candidate suggests a possible problem with this method is encouraging and demonstrates the candidate's grasp of overtime. The answer would gain over half marks.

(d) I think that the order should not be accepted. I have shown that Luxe will make a loss on the order of £5,000 and as limited companies like Luxe try to make as much profit as possible it would be stupid to accept it. Another reason why I think this, is because they normally sell the light for £8.50 so each time they make a new light they will be losing one of their old ones which they would have sold for £1 more. So, in a way they are lucky to be only losing £5,000 and not £6,000 as the new customer wants 6,000 special lights. I can also see from the table that they won't be able to make enough in time for the delivery date. For the first two weeks they have no spare output and only a little from then on. In total they have 5,100 (200 + 500 + 1000 + 1000 + 1200 + 1200) spare which isn't enough. Also, they might get orders at full price from their regular customers between week 3 and week 8 and if they are doing the special order they would have to turn away these customers. This might make them feel angry and never return. To evaluate, there are more bad points than good and so I don't think they should say 'yes'.

🖉 Given the candidate's answer to the question about the total contribution of the new order, the view that the firm will lose money if it accepts the order is entirely understandable. Consequently, when assessing the answer the examiner will work from this (incorrect) position. The candidate offers several reasons to support the view and includes some analysis of other evidence to show that the firm couldn't make the order even if it wanted to. The implied understanding of opportunity cost is good, as is the reference back to the underlying objectives of the firm. The final sentence reflects the fact that the candidate has been taught the need to conclude with evaluation. Unfortunately, this sentence is not evaluative and so the answer remains firmly in L3, analysis, and gains over half marks.

■ ■ ■

Answer to paper 2, question 1: candidate B

(a) Fixed cost per unit means how much it costs to manufacture one unit of whatever it is, in this case electric lights, without taking the variable costs into account. It includes operating costs, labour costs, taxes, electricity and everything that is used in the process of manufacturing and delivering other than raw materials. It is found by dividing the fixed costs by the number of things made, so as more are made it gets smaller.

🖉 Although not as concise as one might expect for a question which assesses under-standing, the candidate nonetheless manages to convey the required depth. Although it is possible to argue that labour costs may not be fixed, the candidate receives the benefit of the doubt. If the candidate had not written the final sentence, then she would not have been answering the whole of the question. Fortunately, this sentence demonstrates appreciation of fixed cost per unit, rather than just fixed cost, and so the examiners can award the majority of the marks.

(b) Contribution = P – VC

Price	=	£7.50
VC = Labour & Materials = £2.50 + £3.50	=	£6.00
Contribution = £7.50 – £6.00	=	£1.50
Total contribution = £1.50 per unit × 6,000 units	=	£9,000

Take away the one-off cost of the new tools.

Total contribution = £9,000 – £5,000	=	£4,000

So the order would make £4,000 contribution.

🖉 This is an exemplary answer in both execution and outcome. It is clearly set out, so it is easy to follow the candidate's method. Further, starting off with a formula shows good technique. The inclusion of the one-off costs for the new tools is a standard feature in examination questions. Normally, contribution is sales revenue minus variable costs. However, as the cost of the new tools only arises because of the order, they need to be taken into account in this instance. This is something the candidate clearly appreciates and full marks would be awarded.

(c) Overtime is the obvious way of doing this. But they could also cut down on maintenance.

> There are two possible methods of achieving a temporary increase in output. However, the question requires more than just identifying methods, as is clear from the key word. As the candidate demonstrates knowledge, it is possible to gain reward at L1.

(d) I think they should accept the order. If they do, they will make an additional £1,000 contribution which will mean profits will rise because I am assuming that they are already paying off all of their fixed costs. Another reason for saying 'yes' is that after doing the order they will already have the special tool, so if the customer comes back they stand to make £6,000 contribution next time. They should do the order and try to persuade the customer to place more orders. Another good point is that by making more lights, the fixed cost per unit will fall from £2.00 because they are spreading their fixed costs over more units and so the profits will rise.

A couple of bad points are that they haven't got the spare capacity to make them from looking at Table 2. But it might be possible to delay some of the planned orders and so squeeze in this new order. Maybe the customers for weeks 7 and 8 won't need their lights until week 9, in which case they could delay the start of these to make the specials. Another problem is that the customers might hear of this special deal at less than the normal price and they might also want the same deal or they will go elsewhere. At £8.50 Luxe make 50p profit per light, but at £7.50 they would make a loss of 50p, which isn't good news.

Whether they accept the order depends on how they read the market. If there is a risk of losing existing customers to rival firms, then they shouldn't take it. But if the new customer might place more orders and Luxe have nothing better to do, it is worth taking as a special one-off introductory offer to show the customer how good they are but then make it clear they want £8.50 from now on.

> Contribution and special orders form an area of the specification that really lends itself to a data–response format. Clearly the candidate has revised this part of the specification and so has been able to include many of the expected factors in the answer. A strong feature of the answer is that the candidate has used the previous parts of the question. For example, the initial question about fixed costs per unit has reminded the candidate that these would fall if output were to rise. Similarly, the discussion of the capital cost of the tools clearly demonstrates that the candidate knows the difference between capital expenditure and revenue expenditure (even if the precise vocabulary is not used).

The answer contains considerations of both sides of the argument and then introduces additional issues. The candidate recognises that there are clear customer relations and marketing issues in these situations. The balance in the discussion is good enough to allow the examiners to award at L4, evaluation, and so the candidate gains the majority of the marks.

■ ■ ■

Question 2

Calculating changes to production

Tom Caxton operates a printing business, Caxton's Printshop Ltd, in the market town of Oakford. Although it is the only business of its sort in the town, he faces competition from other printers in nearby towns. Two major factors determine his competitiveness. The first is the price he quotes. The second is how quickly he can complete the order which, in turn, depends upon how soon he can start the order. If he has the right paper and no other work, he can start immediately. However, other orders or a shortage of paper can cause a delay in starting the job and therefore how soon he could finish it. Tom recognises that failing to complete a job on time causes damage to the reputation of the business.

The business adviser from his bank has suggested to Tom that the adoption of a just-in-time (JIT) approach to the control of stocks of blank paper could save a lot of money. To assess the feasibility of adopting JIT, Tom has collected data about his suppliers' lead-times for his last five orders, as well as for his average daily paper usage for the last 10 weeks. The data appear in Table 1.

Table 1 Lead-time data

Last five orders	Lead-time (days)	Average daily usage per week	
		Week	Units
1	3	1	15
2	2	2	21
3	3	3	16
4	8	4	17
5	4	5	16
		6	17
		7	15
		8	19
		9	17
		10	17

(a) **As the owner of Caxton's Printshop Ltd, Tom enjoys limited liability. Explain what is meant by limited liability.** (4 marks)

(b) **The average lead-time is 4 days. By calculating the mean daily usage, recommend an appropriate reorder level.** (6 marks)

(c) **Outline the factors that Tom should consider before quoting a price for an order.** (4 marks)

(d) **Discuss the advantages and disadvantages of JIT as an approach to stock holding.** (15 marks)

Total: 29 marks

■ ■ ■

Answer to paper 2, question 2: candidate A

(a) Limited liability is when shareholders' liability is limited to the shares they own in the company. If the company were to go bust, the shareholders may lose their shares but are not liable thereafter.

> In answering questions which require the explanation of a term, you should always seek to do so without using the term itself, either in total or part. Here, the candidate has merely suggested that liability is limited, which is not wholly convincing as it lacks development. It would be better to say that the shareholders' responsibility for the debts of the business is confined to the capital they have invested, either through shares or reserves, and, to be strictly accurate, the shareholders have no further personal liability unless the shares they have bought have not yet been fully paid up by them. The candidate would gain half marks for this answer.
>
> The concept of limited liability is one of the fundamental building blocks of business studies. It is the foundation of company formation as a separate entity from its owners and as a legal personality. As such, it is important that you can explain the concept accurately. Further, although it is a concept from the first module, it is highly likely to be examined in other subsequent units.

(b) $170 \div 10 = 17$ each day.
4×17 days $= 68$.
Buffer stock should be 70.

> The answer offered, 70, is not the expected one. The candidate gains credit for the first part of the process in finding the mean daily usage, **17 per day**. However, from here on the answer deteriorates. It is left to the examiner to make the connection that this value has been multiplied by 4 because this is the supplier's lead-time in days. Hence, the reorder level could reasonably be **68 units**. One assumes that the additional two units are just for luck but, as there is no supporting commentary to justify the recommendation, this is far from clear. Note the question requires a recommendation, not merely a calculation.

(c) When setting price, Tom should consider the three Cs of pricing. First he needs to consider his costs so that the price exceeds cost and he can make a profit. Second, he should think about what his competitors will charge and, unless he offers a better service, he has to have a price below or the same as them. Lastly, he needs to consider his customers. If they are desperate they will pay more, but if they have more time he will have to charge less.

> ✓ This is a good answer. Three valid factors are given and each is supported by some commentary. Because the question requires these to be outlined, rather than discussed or explained, a brief sentence about each is adequate. Consequently, this efficient answer gains all of the marks.

(d) There would be both advantages and disadvantages if Tom were to use JIT as an approach to stock holding. The first disadvantage would be that there would be an increased chance of running out of paper. JIT needs reliable suppliers who can deliver the right amount at short notice all of the time. So, when Tom places an order he knows he will get it. The problem is that the supplier can take up to 8 days on one occasion and yet 2 days on another. This would mean it would be very risky to rely on this supplier. Maybe Tom could get them to sign a contract guaranteeing to supply or he should find someone else.

There is also the disadvantage that the goods delivered may not be the ones wanted, or perhaps faulty, which would bring all processes to an entire halt. Although Tom could come to an agreement with the supplier that if this happened he must be paid for the damages, e.g. the loss of business and therefore profit, it would still be damaging to his reputation if he were unable to meet deadlines. It could be disadvantageous if suddenly he was offered a bulk printing order which needed lots of paper and he didn't have it in storage. This would mean the company would appear poorly equipped, damaging its reputation. From the table it is clear that Tom is at some times busier than at others, so if a big order came in, he might not have enough paper because he is now operating JIT which means he has no buffer stock as a safety net. This could lose him business.

JIT is economical in that it saves storage space. Therefore the space that would have been used could host more machines, allowing the company to expand and take on more or different printing orders. Also, because Tom hasn't spent money buying the stock just to sit there, he is saving his cash and only spending it when he really needs to.

Overall, I don't think he should use JIT because he doesn't use the same amount of paper each day and his supplier is too unreliable. If he runs out, then his customers will go to the next town.

> ✓ This is a good answer. The candidate has made sensible use of the data in the question to argue that JIT would not work. (Indeed, the candidate's appreciation of the variability in the usage and lead-time suggests that she rushed the answer to (b) about recommending an appropriate reorder level.) Unusually, and imaginatively, the candidate has shown that there are advantages to JIT which are outweighed by the disadvantages. This shows the ability to evaluate both sides of

the argument and come to a reasoned judgement which can be supported in the context given. Consequently, the candidate gains marks for evaluation at L4 with little difficulty.

■ ■ ■

Answer to paper 2, question 2: candidate B

(a) Limited liability means that someone is not completely liable if the firm in question runs into financial difficulty, for example a shareholder with limited liability could not have their personal finances or assets touched if the business in which they held shares got into debt.

> The candidate manages to convey some appreciation of the concept, but the use of vocabulary is disappointing. Limited liability is not necessarily concerned with the firm getting into debt; rather, it becomes an issue in times of liquidation. The recognition that the owner's risk is confined and that personal assets beyond the investment cannot be seized means the majority of the marks are secured.

(b) Total usage = 170 units in 10 days. They need to reorder when they are about to run out, i.e. lead-time × usage, which gives them enough to use when waiting for a delivery.

	Average	Max	Min
Usage	17	21	15
Lead-time	4	8	2
Reorder	68	168	30

So the reorder level could be anywhere between 168 and 30. Assuming the average is enough, then it is 68.

> The candidate has adopted a rather sophisticated approach to the question and has investigated three different scenarios. The candidate has given a firm recommendation with a supporting commentary. This is a great strength of the answer and helps to demonstrate the candidate's appreciation and understanding that in a dynamic and changing situation the answer given by the average may not be good enough. This answer deserves full marks.

(c) Before quoting a price for a print job, Tom should consider competitors' prices, the materials and type of paper and ink required, and the current demand.

> Here the candidate has explicitly identified one factor, competitors' prices, and implied another factor, costs. These are not developed to say how they might influence Tom's pricing decision and so it is not clear what bearing the competition would have. As such, the answer demonstrates knowledge and would be rewarded at L1.

(d) The just-in-time approach to stock holding has many advantages. It would give Tom's firm a stronger link with suppliers if a suitable supplier can be found. I don't think the supplier he has is good enough as the lead-time changes so much from 2 days to 8 days. If Tom did use JIT, this would not be good enough as the supplier has to be reliable. If there were problems with the supplier, then Tom's business will run out of stock very quickly which means he will have to turn business away or ask the customer to wait, which they might not be willing to do. The other disadvantage of using JIT is that he might no longer get economies of scale when ordering paper because he is ordering smaller amounts but more often. This might mean his costs go up, so he has to raise his prices.

On the other hand, JIT may cut costs in stock holding and improve the efficiency of the firm. This might allow him to reduce prices so he becomes more competitive. Another advantage of JIT is that he won't have lots of stock sitting around. This might be OK for white paper but he wouldn't want loads of stocks of different colours taking up lots of space and tying up lots of his capital.

The candidate has discussed both advantages and disadvantages as is required by the question. The candidate has also tried to place the answer into the context given. This is a good feature and clearly lifts the quality of the answer above application at L2. It is therefore a pity that the strong discussion does not have an overall and final summary, to come to a view about whether the advantages outweigh the disadvantages, or vice versa. In the absence of evaluation, the answer is therefore rewarded as analysis at L3, but at the upper end of this mark range.

Candidate A would gain a C grade. If the answer to the questions about Luxe had been as good as those to questions about Caxton's, then a higher grade would have been achieved. It would be appropriate to compare and contrast this candidate's two answers and identify the differences between them. The answers to the Caxton questions are clearly of A-grade standard, although maximum marks were only achieved for the question about the factors Tom should consider before quoting a price.

Candidate B had no difficulties with the two numerical questions on the paper, scoring highly on both. This performance was supported by two good discursive answers to the major, final part questions. This positive feature enables the examiners to award an A grade. Note that the script is far from perfect, but the examiner recognises that the time pressures in an examination mean that perfection is neither likely nor required.

Question 1

Determining cash flow

Sachin Bhatia operates a private hire taxi business, A2B4U. Sachin and his father are the only investors in the business, but Sachin is in day-to-day control because his father is too busy running his own businesses. Sachin runs the business as he sees fit and does not need to publish accounts because the Bhatias are the only owners. Both Sachin and his father welcome this degree of business confidentiality.

One of Sachin's main concerns is ensuring the business has an appropriate level of cash in its bank account. This is for two reasons. First, he has unlimited liability. Second, being a small business, A2B4U does not have the luxury of spare financial resources. To help ensure the firm's finance is optimised, Sachin constructs a quarterly cash flow forecast. This is given in Table 1. It is Sachin's belief that A2B4U will be successful provided it has enough cash and its vehicles are in use. He takes this approach to minimise his risk. A garage owned by Sachin's father maintains all of the firm's vehicles at a very competitive rate. Drivers are employed on a part-time basis.

Table 1 The A2B4U cash flow (£)

	June	July	August
Cash sales	1,200	1,080	
Sales on account	750	800	720
Total sales	1,950	1,880	
Wages	600	600	600
Fuel	700	630	
Salary	500	500	500
Overhead	100	100	100
Total outflow	1,900	1,830	
Net cash flow	50	50	
Opening cash	300	350	
Closing cash	350	400	

About 40% of business is from account customers. These customers are invoiced at the end of each month and they are expected to pay within 30 days. Although it is rare for the business to have difficulties collecting debts, this has happened in the past.

(a) Giving your reasons, identify the legal structure of A2B4U. (4 marks)

(b) Calculate A2B4U's cash for the end of August on the assumption that August sales are £2,500, fuel is 35% of monthly sales and a £400 maintenance invoice is to be paid. (6 marks)

(c) An account customer has been declared insolvent. It owes A2B4U £500, which was to be paid in September. Explain the effect of this on both the cash and profit position in September. (4 marks)

(d) Discuss appropriate methods Sachin might use to minimise the risks of operating A2B4U. (15 marks)

Total: 29 marks

■ ■ ■

Answer to paper 3, question 1: candidate A

(a) I think A2B4U is a partnership because only two owners are mentioned. Also we are told they don't publish accounts and that Sachin has unlimited liability which are two other things which apply to partnerships.

🖉 The candidate has identified a valid legal structure. However, the reasoning in the first sentence is weak in that it is equally true for a limited company. As such, it is not as convincing as the reasons given in the second sentence. Overall, the candidate has given a legal structure and reasons and so would be rewarded for application at L2.

(b) Cash sales = 60% of £2,500 = £1,500
Credit sales = £720
Cash inflow = £2,220
Fuel is 35% of £2,500 = £875
Other costs are £1,200
Cash outflow = £2,075
Net cash for month = £145
Opening cash = £400, so closing cash is £545.

🖉 The candidate does not achieve the anticipated answer and so it is necessary to follow the method. Fortunately, the method is generally good so it is clear that the mark for cash outflow cannot be awarded because the payment of the garage bill has been overlooked. This results in the cash outflow being £400 short. However, because no other error was made, the final answer is consistent with the incorrect cash outflow. This allows the examiner to award the other intermediate marks. The learning points are that it is essential to show all workings and method and to read the entire question very carefully as this may also contain vital data which you can incorporate in the answer.

(c) If the customer can't pay, then the cash position for September will be down by this amount because the firm was expecting it in September. There is no impact on the profit position for September as the money was earned in August and so it would have been included in the August profit calculation. To be accurate, Sachin should deduct the £500 from the August P&L account. Otherwise he will think he has made more profit than he really has.

The candidate enjoys a clear understanding of the differences between cash flow and profit. One of the key differences is that cash reflects the actual timing of receipts of income, whereas profit is recorded in the month the revenue is earned, regardless of whether the revenue is then paid in cash or held as a debtor with the cash to be paid later. The answer is correct and so maximum marks can be awarded.

(d) Sachin should turn the business into a limited company so that he can have limited liability. This means he is only liable for the amount of money he has put into the business and cannot lose his personal assets. But setting up a limited company takes time and money that his father might not be willing to spend. Also a company has to publish its accounts and so anyone can see how they are doing. This might help a rival firm against them. Since they want to keep their affairs secret, a limited company might not be the best solution. Another thing he could do is to make his father an active partner in the business and become an employee, so that he is a sleeping partner. If he can't do this, then he needs to run the business better, so that it doesn't run into problems. So maybe he could stop doing account work as this is risky because the account might be unpaid at the end of the month. This would leave the business short of money as Sachin will have paid wages to the drivers but not taken in enough money.

What he does depends on what he wants. If he is really determined to minimise his risk, then I think he should become a limited company. But if secrecy is more important, then he will just have to accept the risk. It could be that he can't do anything as his father has to be consulted and he might not see any problem as he has limited liability already. If so, Sachin will just have to accept it. After all, you have to speculate to accumulate.

It is the second paragraph that contains the most effective part of the answer. The candidate has reasoned that the solution is dependent upon the objectives of the owner and has recognised that these objectives are in conflict with each other. Consequently, the course of action becomes clear once the owner has decided which objective is paramount. The realisation that Sachin's father might be a barrier to any action is good. Overall, the answer is evaluative and so gains access to the top level of evaluation at L4.

■ ■ ■

Answer to paper 3, question 1: candidate B

(a) A partnership is defined by the Partnership Act as two or more people carrying on a business together with a view to profit. This seems to be the case here and so I would say it is a partnership. Other reasons which support this are that partnerships don't have to publish annual accounts and that at least one owner has to have unlimited liability. As Sachin's father doesn't take any decisions, he is a sleeping partner which means Sachin has unlimited liability.

✐ This is a very good answer that gains top marks. The answer demonstrates clearly the candidate's understanding of legal structures. The only possible criticism is that it is rather long.

(b) Cash in: £2,500 + £720 = £3,320
Cash out: £600 + £875 + £500 + £100 + £400 = £2,475
So cash = £845

✐ The answer given, £845, is not the one expected and so full marks are not awarded. To determine the mark for this question, it is necessary to follow the candidate's method. The mark for monthly cash sales cannot be awarded because the candidate has treated all sales as cash rather than just 60% of them. However, a mark is awarded for the total cash inflow because this is consistent with the earlier error. The value for fuel is correct and so this mark is awarded, as is the mark for cash outflow because the garage invoice has been included. Overall, 3 marks are awarded.

(c) Both cash and profit will be down by £500 because the customer can't pay. Sachin might decide not to have account customers just in case they can't pay or maybe he could get them to pay up front and then he could deduct their fares from their accounts so if they go bust he isn't short of money.

✐ Only half marks can be awarded because the statement about profit is incorrect. The suggestion about how this situation could be avoided is interesting but not rewardable because it was not asked for in the question. The learning point is to answer the question set and not to waste time offering material that isn't needed. No marks are deducted for this extra material, as the penalty paid is the additional time it took the candidate to write it.

(d) Risk in business cannot be avoided in full and so Sachin will have to accept some. What he can do is to minimise this but still be able to make a profit because this is the owners' reward for taking risk. What he could do is to run his company so that he has as few fixed costs as possible so that when times aren't good he doesn't have a lot to pay out. Fixed costs are costs which don't vary with output. The other costs are variable costs which go up with the amount of business. He could lower fixed costs by selling his cabs to the workers so that he doesn't have to pay the maintenance, tax, insurance etc. He might have to pay each driver more for each journey, but at least he wouldn't have to pay out when he doesn't have much business. What he is doing is linking his payments to the drivers with the business he is taking in. This means that unless a fare wasn't paid and he charges more than his costs, he should always run the company at a profit and so he isn't at risk. The only risk he then has is that account holders don't pay up. But I have already said how he could avoid this by having a voucher system. The only snag is that 40% of his business is from accounts so if there are other cab companies, then he might lose trade.

✐ The majority of the marks are awarded here as the answer contains analysis. The consideration of cost structure is certainly one way of reducing business risk and so is rewardable. The discussion of types of cost demonstrates the candidate's understanding of this aspect of the specification. The consequences of the possible change in cost structure are explored quite well.

It is worth noting the candidate's poor grasp of vocabulary. In the question which demanded analysis of A2B4U's legal structure, the business is described as a partnership, yet throughout this answer it is referred to as a company. This seemingly small oversight detracts from the quality of the answer and is an error that should be avoided.

■ ■ ■

Question 2

Workforce planning

Chris Choi is employed as Director of Human Resources at Paddock and Kane Ltd. The local economy of the town is healthy and there is very little local unemployment. Chris is currently concerned about the company's ability to attract suitable new staff. This is of particular concern given the fall in the number of school leavers and other demographic changes shown in Table 1.

Table 1 UK labour force by age (millions)

	16–24	25–44	45–54	55+
1971	5.3	10.0	5.3	5.1
1981	5.9	11.7	5.1	4.2
1991	5.7	14.2	5.4	3.5
2001*	4.5	14.6	6.4	3.8
2011*	5.1	13.5	7.5	4.4
*Estimated				

Table 2 Monthly demand for BR545

January	2,500
February	2,520
March	2,560
April	2,650
May	2,660
June	2,700
July	2,780
August	2,700
September	2,660
October	2,560
November	2,500
December	2,410

Monthly demand for one of the company's products, BR545, is shown in Table 2. Three production employees are needed to make BR545 and the standard manufacturing time is 20 minutes. There is some variation between standard time and actual time. Manufacturing workers are employed for a 40-hour week, but Chris assumes they actually work 34 hours per week because of rest breaks. In a typical month, an employee would work 22 days.

(a) **Outline the main features of workforce planning.** (4 marks)

(b) **Calculate the number of employees required to meet the average monthly demand for BR545.** (6 marks)

(c) **Using Table 1, calculate the change between 1971 and 2011 in the proportion of the UK labour force that is less than 25 years old.** (4 marks)

(d) **Discuss how Paddock and Kane can ensure it has the appropriate number of employees.** (15 marks)

Total: 29 marks

■ ■ ■

Answer to paper 3, question 2: candidate A

(a) Workforce planning is when the managers of the business sit down with the workers and plan what they are going to do. This means the business will be run more efficiently because everyone knows what he or she has to do and so fewer mistakes will be made and fewer things will be wasted.

🖉 Unfortunately this answer contains nothing that is rewardable. The candidate has not demonstrated knowledge of workforce planning within the meaning in the specification. As L1 cannot be awarded, the answer gains zero marks.

(b) Average demand = total demand ÷ months = 31,200 ÷ 12 = 2,600 per month
One unit needs 3 staff × 20 minutes each
So, one unit requires one man-hour and needs 2,600 man-hours each month
One worker does 34 hours week × 22 days = 748 man-hours per month
Monthly manning level = 2,600 ÷ 748 = 3.48 employees

🖉 The candidate has demonstrated good examination technique in setting out the answer logically and clearly. Interestingly, although the candidate cannot explain what manpower planning is, he is able to engage in a typical calculation associated with this aspect of the specification. He has been able to calculate the demand for labour in man-hours. This is derived from the demand for the product. Similarly, the candidate is able to determine the supply of labour, again in man-hours, provided by one employee. Combining the two gives the manning level required. It is worth noting that manning levels need not be in whole numbers of employees. The answer is correct and deserves full marks.

(c) 1971 5.3 ÷ 25.7 = 20.6%
2011 5.1 ÷ 30.5 = 16.7%
Change is −18.9%

🖉 Here the candidate has assumed the examiner wants the change as a percentage (it could be argued that it is not entirely clear what form the examiner wants the answer in). Given this interpretation, it is pleasing that the candidate has not merely subtracted one value from the other to achieve 3.9%. Similarly, it is good that the minus sign is included as this shows that the proportion has gone down. Full marks are awarded.

(d) Paddock and Kane, P&K, can do various things to ensure it has the appropriate number of employees. First, it can recruit them, having worked out how many it needs. The way it recruits would depend upon what it is they are making and whether the workers need to be skilled. They might put an advert in the local paper or they could phone the job centre if the skill isn't too high. Or they might want to train their own workers who work somewhere else in the factory. Another thing they could do is to make the workers work longer by cutting down their breaks. This would mean they wouldn't need as many, but I don't think the workers would like this and so there might be trouble. If they can't make them work for longer, then they might be able to make them work faster by motivating them. They could use Herzberg's two-factor theory and make sure the hygiene is good so that the workers are motivated. Or they could pay them for each unit they make and so they would work faster according to Taylor but, if they did this, they would have to inspect for quality. One problem they have is that demand for BR545 changes and so the amount of work each worker has to do will change with the months. Although they need 3.5 workers on average, this will be too many in December and too few in June. Maybe they need to use part-time staff.

🖉 The candidate begins by suggesting a number of methods and these are loosely related to the situation. As such, the answer is demonstrating the skill of application. The inclusion of human resources management (HRM) theory is promising but not developed to the depth required. However, the eventual recognition that the firm faces variable demand is good and the suggested means of ensuring they have enough employees is sound. It is this analysis that allows for the bulk of the marks to be awarded for analysis at L3.

■ ■ ■

Answer to paper 3, question 2: candidate B

(a) There are two features of workforce planning. One is the demand for workers. The company will work out what their orders are going to be in the future and how long it takes to make their products. This means they know how many workers they will need once they have allowed for holidays and other days off. Then the company looks at how many workers it has and compares this to how many it needs. If it hasn't got enough it can plan what it is going to do. It might decide to recruit new staff or to train them so they are better.

🖉 The candidate demonstrates good understanding of the term. The explanation is sound, although not especially well executed. For example, the candidate says there are two features but then fails to identify explicitly what the second is (the supply of labour). It might be tempting to think that the explanation could offer more detail, but the key verb in the question is 'outline', something the candidate has done, and so this answer gains full marks.

(b) Average demand is: $\dfrac{2{,}500 + 2{,}410}{2}$ = 2,455 each month

It takes 20 minutes to make one unit, so a worker can make three each hour:
2,455 ÷ 3 = 818.33 hours
One person works 34 hours each week
So it needs 6.02 workers which means 6 workers with them doing slightly more hours each week

🖉 There are several problems with this answer. First, the outcome is incorrect. Second, the candidate has skipped several stages in some calculations. The only credit that can be awarded is for the final value of 6.02. However, it is left for the examiner to determine this by dividing the apparent need for labour, 818.33 by the candidate's interpretation of supply, 34 man-hours per week x 4 weeks (818.33 ÷ 136 = 6.02). One mark can be awarded.

(c) In 1971 there were 5.3 million in the workforce, but in 2011 this has gone down to 5.1 million. The difference is 0.2 million over 40 years, so that is 5,000 per year.

🖉 The candidate has not answered the question. There are various concerns about the answer. First, the candidate has not recognised the need to use relative values rather than absolutes. Second, the calculation undertaken is not the one required. No marks are awarded.

(d) The company needs just enough workers to do the job but not too many, otherwise it will have costs which are too high and so lower profits. The way they can ensure they have enough workers is to use workforce planning by seeing how many they need and compare this to how many they have. If there is a difference, they could either fire a few, if they have too many, or hire more if they haven't got enough. But firing workers might cause labour problems, so it might be better to allow the number of workers they have to fall through natural wastage. This means that when a worker leaves, either to get another job or retire, they aren't replaced. Although it might take some time to get down to the right number, it would be better for worker morale and so production. But a problem with this is that the people who are left might not have the right qualifications for the job and so new workers would still need to be hired. Another thing they could do is to hire new workers. Because the number of young workers is falling as calculated in the question before, they might be better off trying to find older workers as there are more of these. For example, the 45–54 group is growing. By going for these workers they will be cheaper as there are more of them. The method they use really depends on how big the problems is and weather they need to hire or fire. Having temporary staff will be good for a short time but not for a long time. So they need to know how long they are going to be with the wrong numbers of staff.

📝 Despite the grammatical and spelling errors, this is a good answer. The candidate clearly understands workforce planning and is able to discuss features of it. The attempt to use the data in the question is good and the comment made about the falling age profile of under 25s is interesting. It is a pity that this point was not more fully reasoned as more marks would have been awarded if the consequence had been explored in greater depth. Remember, you gain marks for the depth of your discussion, so a few well-made points are better than several merely identified. Overall, the answer would gain access to L3.

📝 **Despite a relatively poor grasp of workforce planning, Candidate A's performance in the A2B4U questions is enough to compensate and still achieve an overall A grade. This is in no small part assisted by two factors: first, the evaluation in the last A2B4U question; second, the high marks gained for the calculations. The pattern of marks shows that it is vital to be able to answer numerical calculations as well as demonstrate the skill of evaluation.**

Candidate B enjoys good understanding of the subject and scores well on those questions only requiring a L2 response. The performance is hampered by weak numerate skills and a failure to engage in evaluation. Another weakness is the relatively poor quality of written communication that would prevent the awarding of top marks for this aspect of the assessment. Overall, this performance would gain a C grade.